"Just finished reading the latest draft of THIRTY CENTS AN ACRE and found it delightful. Very interesting, educational, and, most of all, definitely not a dry tome of facts and figures. "Since my college days, when I had a history professor who truly made history live, I have hated many of those dry tomes of facts and figures that abound. I realize the authors worked hard on research and wanted to give all the information to generations then and now, but I have always felt they could have done so in a more interesting manner. You have done it and made it live for your readers.

"Thanks for sharing with your wonderful talent!"

--CAROLYN CARSON, CURATOR,
WESTON HISTORY MUSEUM

"I thought your narrative was very fast-paced and compelling, conversational in a way, and I have no quarrels with your interpretations and broad-based grasp of facts whatsoever. I also enjoyed your geographical references which I felt really helped place the narrative in a concrete place and time. Great stuff."

--BRENT RUTHERFORD, ELAM BROWN'S
GREAT-GREAT-GREAT-GRANDSON

"What a fascinating story and presentation you have put together. Great job on the research!"

--TAMI (ALLEN) MULLINS,
ELAM BROWN'S GREAT-GREAT-
GREAT-GREAT-GREAT
STEP-GRANDAUGHTER

THIRTY CENTS AN ACRE expertly fills in many historical gaps in the life of Elam Brown and brings him vividly to life. You have connected the personal aspects of Brown's life with the historical details of the time period in a thought-provoking way."

--MARY McCOSKER, PRESIDENT,
LAFAYETTE HISTORICAL SOCIETY

THIRTY CENTS AN ACRE is a compelling, clearly presented and thoroughly researched book. Mr. Peters has found the perfect family to serve as its focus for they appear to have been involved in very many important activities as related to the settlement of the West. I learned a great deal from the manuscript and enjoyed it from the first page to the last, including its detailed bibliography."

--WILLIAM J. URICCHIO,
UNIVERSITY OF CONNECTICUT
ASSOCIATE LIBRARIAN (RETIRED)

THIRTY CENTS AN ACRE
A Lafayette Odyssey

Ray Peters

Published by BookLocker.com, Inc., St. Petersburg, Florida, U.S.A.

Printed on acid-free paper.

BookLocker.com, Inc.
2017

First Edition

…Western expansion began not in America, but in Europe…

(Hubert Howe Bancroft, 1832-1918)

Dedicated to Brent Rutherford

Historia Extraordinarius

A great-great-great grandson of Elam Brown.

Brent vetted this volume

Which he promised to someday read to his granddaughter.

Sorry we didn't finish in time, Brent

Ray Peters

ACKNOWLEDGMENTS

Gloria Boyer, Platte County Recorder of Deeds; **Michael Chamofsky,** East Bay Regional Parks District History Resources; **James S. Clayton,** Multnomah County Surveyor; **Carl R. Clinton,** Clackamus County Surveyor; **Brian Henson,** Survey Supervisor, Multnomah County Surveyor's Office; **Jennifer Keyser,** Oregon Historical Society; **Linda Knitter,** The State Bar of California; **Carolyn Larson,** Curator, Weston Historical Museum; **David L. McFadden,** President California Supreme Court Historical Society; **Brent Rutherford,** Elam Brown's Great-Great-Great Grandson; **Captain Jack Fiorito,** Landmarks History Collection; **David M. Gotz~***Archivist,* Belvedere-Tiburon Landmarks Society; **Don Bertolette,** President, Western Native Tree Society; **Dorothy Mutnick,** Author, *Some California Poppies & Even a Few Mommies;* **Nilda Rego,** Historical Columnist, *Contra Costa Times;* **Mary McCosker,** President, Lafayette Historical Society; **Charles Chase Venegas,** Contra Costa County Library; **David Peterson,** Brent Rutherford's cousin; **Tami (Allen) Mullins,** Elam & Margaret Brown's Great-Great-Great-Great Step-Granddaughter; **Adam Nilsen,** Author, *City of Pleasant Hill,* **Denise Koroslev,** President, Friends of the Rodgers Ranch; **Dean McLeod,** Contra Costa County Historical Society; **Ann Merideth,** City of Lafayette; **Priscilla A. Couden,** Executive Director, Contra Costa County Historical Society; **Laura Dorsey Huerta,** Executive Assistant, Contra Costa County Office of Education; **Joanne Robbins,** City

Clerk, City of Lafayette; The Bancroft Library, University of California; **Louise Pubols,** Senior Curator of History, Oakland Museum of CA; **Gregory Watz,** Utah State Historical Society; **Steve Beck,** Sutter's Fort State Historic Park; **Donald Pohlman,** Oakland Museum of CA; **Judy Russo,** Registrar, Sacramento History and Railroad Sector, California State Parks; **Bill Oudegeest,** Donner Summit Historical Society; **John C. Evanoff,** VisitReno; **Mary Ranelletti,** descendant of the Brown, Smith, Allen, and Bradley families; **Jim Stein,** Contra Costa County Surveyor.

COMMEMORATION

"There is a class of topographical engineers older than the schools and more unerring than the mathematics. They are the wild animals-buffalo, elk, deer, antelope, bears-which traverse the forested not by compass but by an instinct that leads them always the right way to the lowest passes in the mountains, the shallowest fords in the river-and the shortest practicable lines between remote points. A buffalo path becomes a warpath...and finally the macadamized or railroad of the scientific man. Creeks or rivers, of course, are easy guides: one can quickly reliably determine from the flow which of the two directions is indicated: up or down."

Cong. Globe, 30 Cong., 2 Sess., 25, 388.472; Thomas Hart Benton, *Highway to the Pacific,* 1850.

TABLE OF CONTENTS

PROLOGUE xv

ONE - New England 1797-1804 1

TWO - Ohio 1804-1818 9

THREE - Missouri 1818-1819 36

FOUR - Illinois Madison County 1819-1836 39

FIVE - The Platte 1836-1843 56

SIX - THOMAS 1843-1846 78

SEVEN - WESTON 1845-1846 96

EIGHT - FORT JOHN [LARAMIE] APRIL-
    JUNE 1846 110

NINE - BRIDGER'S FORT
    JUNE-JULY 1846 124

TEN - FORT HALL JULY-AUGUST 1846 135

ELEVEN - JESSE 1843-1846 143

TWELVE - APPLEGATE'S TRAIL AUGUST-
    SEPTEMBER 1846 159

THIRTEEN - [ROLLER PASS]
    OCTOBER, 1846 175

FOURTEEN - JOHNSON'S RANCH
    OCTOBER, 1846 181

FIFTEEN - SUTTER'S FORT
    OCTOBER 1846 189

SIXTEEN - SAN JOSE October-
    November 1846 206

SEVENTEEN - BATTLE OF SANTA CLARA
1846-1847 214

EIGHTEEN - The Greatest Trees
February 1847 236

NINETEEN - Benicia August 1847 247

TWENTY - *El Diseño* [The Map] August 1847-
February 1848 256

TWENTY-ONE - *Nous voila, Lafayette!* [Lafayette,
We Are Here!] January-February 1848 265

AFTERWORD 268

SELECTED BIBLIOGRAPHY 271

PROLOGUE

1759, August 1: The first shot of The American Revolutionary War is fired in Prussia during the Seven Years' War at the Battle of Minden; the shot killed a French colonel aux Grenadiers de France. *An extraordinary chain of events is set into motion...*

The French colonel had a two-year-old son who, because of the typical exigencies of the military, had never seen his father. And, because of an Englishman's bullet, he never would. Later, when the boy asked why he had no apparent father, he was told about the Englishman, for it was far simpler to blame that enemy of the French than to explain the Seven Years' War. Eventually, in the mind's eye of the small boy, the image of that loathsome Englishman grew until it had achieved ogre-like proportions. Soon, *all* Englishmen would look like that monster. As the paradox of a simple horseshoe that grew to the loss of a kingdom in the ancient proverb *For Want of a Nail,* the musket ball had become an enormous cannonball threatening life and limb. By the age of ten, the boy loathed all things English.

His name was Marie-Joseph Paul Yves Roch Gilbert du Motier, quite a cumbersome title for a little boy. His mother called him "Gilbert."

Gilbert's mother and great-grandfather both died when the boy was thirteen, which unfortunate circumstances left him with only a wealthy grandfather as a living relative. It is ironic that a the great-grandfather had once owned a very large estate. By a continuance of rapid strokes of fate, Gilbert was destined to become one of the richest persons in all of France.

He still hated the English. It was inevitable that, having had a colonel as a father, the boy would be interested in joining the military, especially since the military, in all probability, might provide him with an opportunity to set things to rights about his father's death. He joined up on April 9, 1771.

He was only fourteen in 1771, but that would not be a problem for one destined to become one of the richest people in France. In full accordance with standard procedures at the time, and with the help of that wealthy grandfather, he bought a commission in the *Black Musketeers* and was immediately commissioned as an officer.

Wealth had made it easy for him to become a commissioned officer. However: if one desired to advance in the military, wealth alone would not do: one also needed connections. His socially prominent grandfather was there to help: within two years arranging a marriage to the enchanting Adrienne, a fourteen-year-old offspring of the powerful Noailles family. The military career of this sixteen year old officer looked to be firmly established.

However, unsettling difficulties began to appear. Gilbert's fellow officers disliked him: they called him incompetent, naïve, indecisive, bumbling, inexperienced, hopelessly unattractive, altogether awkward, dull and inferior. After all, he *was* the youngest member of the troop. In spite of great wealth and great connections, his glorious military career came to a sudden and humiliating end on June 11, 1776, when he found himself on the inactive list.

However, as often happens in life, a new bright star shines just when one finds himself marooned in the bottom of a pit. News arrived in France that a handful of so-called "Americans" had declared themselves to be independent of England! No sooner had that glorious announcement presented itself when it was further announced that these impertinent "Americans" were anxious to recruit French military officers!

Gilbert at once approached the American envoy to France, an energetic operator named Silas Deane. The delighted Deane noted Gilbert's resplendently decorated *Black Musketeers* uniform. Unaware that this splendid young man was on the inactive list, the envoy eagerly offered a contract to obtain the glittering French officer for the American cause.

At that moment, neither Silas Deane nor Gilbert knew that the Americans had very recently suffered a major defeat in the Battle of Long Island. The French government had, as a result, forbidden any of their officers to join the Americans. Undaunted, with the pledge of a commission as a major general in his hand and a bulging wallet in his pocket, Gilbert purchased a ship. The little vessel, fittingly named *Victoire,* set sail from Bordeaux on April 20, 1777 with Gilbert and other would-be American officers aboard.

They were stunned upon their arrival at Philadelphia when told that the ubiquitous Silas Deane had no authority to offer American commissions to the French officers, and that they must return to France forthwith. With the temerity of a nineteen-year-old, Gilbert presented letters of introduction indicating that he really wanted to fight and was not an arrogant foreigner, but a gentleman with a polite demeanor. He asked only for a chance to prove himself. Furthermore, he would be willing to serve without pay. *As a major general, of course.*

The matter went to the Congress. At this point, the nation was impoverished. Congress accepted his terms and passed a resolution on July 31, 1777 reading in part: *"...that in consideration of his zeal, his illustrious family, and connexions (sic), he have the rank and commission of a major general in the army of the United States."*

Never again would Gilbert be labeled "incompetent, naïve, indecisive, etc." He was taken to meet General George Washington, who welcomed Gilbert as the son he had never had. And the new major general found the father he had never had.

His first blood for the American cause was shed at the Battle of Brandywine, for which he was cited by General Washington for "bravery and military ardour (sic)." No longer dull, tongue-tied, and inferior, he gloriously marched on to fight valiantly in the Battles of Lafayette Hill, Gloucester, Monmouth, Rhode Island, and Green Spring.

But a successful army needs more than valor: it also needs such everyday articles as food, clothing, blankets, tents, guns, ammunition, and bandages, all of which were in very short supply in the Continental Army. Gilbert took a temporary respite from the fighting: On January 11, 1779, he sailed back to France aboard the frigate *Alliance* in search of assistance. Things didn't go well: upon arrival at Lorient on February 6, he was put under house arrest because of his defiance of the French government's order not to join the American forces. However, on February 14, 1779, the French Foreign Minister received a letter from none other than Benjamin Franklin, which expressed the highest esteem for the Marquis de La Fayette. On February 19, Gilbert himself wrote a letter to King Louis XVI to apologize for his earlier disobedience. The King at once invited this vaunted American major general to a levee (reception).

Lafayette became the toast of Paris. He reciprocated by buying an entire regiment of the King's Dragoons which he (delightedly) offered to lead in a planned conquest of England by the French army, to be followed by an expeditionary force to America.

The weather took a turn for the worse; the proposed invasion of England had been abandoned. Better news arrived from Adrienne: on December 24, she had given birth to a son. Gilbert promptly named him "George Washington," and it was said that General Washington was most gratified by the honor.

However, bad news began to arrive from America: money, food, clothing, weapons and ammunition were sadly lacking. Lafayette contacted the French Minister of War and requested 40,000 guns and the powder to go with them. He triumphantly returned to America by the King's order on March 6, 1780 as a representative of France, arriving in Boston to a tremendous reception. Grateful tears rolled down Washington's cheeks when he heard that 6,000 infantrymen would soon arrive, along with abundant supplies of arms, clothing, and ammunition. *And the French fleet!*

The effusive Marquis then received further word from King Louis XVI that France had become fully committed to the American cause and would fight on with them until the thirteen states were independent from Great Britain. Thus emboldened, Major General Lafayette moved his force to Chesapeake Bay to provoke a battle with British General Cornwallis.

Washington, aware of two French fleets sailing southerly, instructed Lafayette to remain in place to block a possible land escape by Cornwallis while the French bottled up the Bay to ward off an approaching British fleet.

The French fleets converged on Yorktown and were in position by at the end of August: twenty-eight ships of the line, six frigates, twenty-one hundred marines, eighteen hundred sailors and eight cannon.

Things were looking up.

Until the curse of the *miasma* struck the Marquis.

Miserably ill, he dragged himself from bed to greet General Washington, the welcome French marines, and the enormous collection of forty friendly ships. Long tables were set up in large tents and much food was found. The commanders, French and American, exuberantly exchanged numerous toasts and considerable praise. General Washington reviewed the combined forces, who responded with numerous musket salutes.

Cornwallis and his men must have stared with awe at the massive French fleets. Their egos must have been shattered by the noisy carousing, the repeated volleys of celebratory musket salutes. They must have felt a great foreboding at the sight of the advancing hordes of men carrying shovels for the digging of trenches all around their encampment.

The attack began on October 6.

After only thirteen days, the signature battle of the Revolutionary War had ended.

It is said the bands played *The World Turned Upside Down* at 2:00 PM on October 19, 1780, when the vanquished British army, until that moment considered the most powerful in all the world, marched out of Yorktown. When the red-coated soldiers made a point of looking to the French soldiers as if they were surrendering to them, Lafayette ordered his band to raise the volume of *Yankee Doodle* to full blast. The British turned back to face the Americans.

ONE

New England

1797-1804

Down in the new city of Washington, the *President's House* wasn't yet finished. In Boston, a very respectable forty-four gun frigate not yet named the *USS Constitution* lay on her ways, still unfinished, not to be launched for another six months. The second President of the United States, John Adams, had been on his new job for merely three months. George Washington, that first and most highly revered first President, at last had begun to settle into a quiet retirement on his farm at Mt. Vernon.

The retired President (and General) had had his mind filled to overflowing, what with all the work to be done on the long-neglected farm. The war with England and the *Startup Country* (now called the United States) had consumed his thought-processes for too long a period of time. Although construction of the *President's House* might have once interfered with their plans, both George and Martha considered themselves fortunate that they had nothing to do with the floor plan or the size of the kitchen. Indeed, the former President was so absorbed in the catchup work on the farm that he was totally unaware of a significant event then taking place on June 10, 1797, way up in Herkimer County, New York.

On that date Mrs. Elizabeth Lynds Brown gave birth to a little boy.

She named him "Elam."

Elam's mother was thought to have been an American, although America hadn't yet been in existence when she was born in Spencer, Worcester County, Massachusetts, on February 2, 1768. Since Massachusetts was then a colony of (Old) England, it was, of course English, even if in America.

Elizabeth's folks, therefore, had merely emigrated from the old part of England to the new. It can be seen that this all could become very confusing, for the people in the new part of England spoke with the same accents as those that stayed behind in the old part. In fact, it became so confusing that the two places would fight another war fifteen years later, in 1812, because the peoples in the two Englands couldn't tell each other apart. (Or so they would say.)

But "New England" was, of course, in the "New World," while "Old England," then called, simply, "England," remained in the "Old World," across the Atlantic. England fought the "American War" at the same time the Americans fought the "Revolutionary War," to completely confuse future historians.

Elam's father was named "Thomas Brown," and had an addition to his name of "the estimable," so his full name became "The Estimable Thomas Brown," for reasons to be cited later in this dissertation. Since The Estimable Thomas Brown was male, he therefore played a minor role in the actual birthing, as the process was then called.

The Estimable Thomas Brown was born on November 28, 1769 in Berkshire Hill, Massachusetts, and might be considered to be native American, which theory was heartily contradicted by his parents, who emphatically avowed that they had come from Scotland before there *was* an America. And because Massachusetts at the time was a British colony (or "Scottish," depending on which parent you listened to) both of the Browns stubbornly insisted that Elam was Scottish (or English).

In any case, whether English, Scottish, British or American, Elam's parents had married on February 8, 1791, which action, in all probability, didn't stop the squabbling. (Squabbling between the Scots and the English had already been going on for so many centuries it couldn't be expected to stop because of a mere wedding.)

Whatever the nationality, it was nevertheless obvious that little Elam had been born with the genes of wanderers. *As such, Elam became a bit of a wanderer himself.*

Berkshire County, Massachusetts
1798

The Browns remained in Herkimer County a mere six months after Elam's birthing, for, at the age of twenty-nine, his father became restless. He had been repeatedly stressing to Elizabeth that the soil in Herkimer County, already full of rocky quartz when they arrived, was getting even rockier. Every time he plowed the fields, he insisted, new rocks rose to the surface, and the new rocks were bigger and heavier than the old rocks. It was a fact, he recalled, that this phenomenon had not been evident back where he had grown up in Massachusetts. Elizabeth, at last tiring of the daily tirade about big rising rocks, finally weakened and suggested they move to Massachusetts. *Where gorgeous rock walls encircled all the fields.*

The growth of restlessness might also have been partially caused by the new-born son, now growing older. As the son grew, the father noticed that the furrows he plowed in the fields appeared to get a little longer each day, in spite of the fact that he remained a young man. His pitchfork, even when not fully loaded with hay, likewise appeared to be getting heavier. After a long day plowing longer furrows and pitching heavier hay, minor back-aches become significantly achier.

However, Thomas considered that since he now had a son, he could expect a significant difference: improvement to his aching back. Before Elam, his wife had had only girls: Eliza, born January 28. 1790, and Sophronia, February 15, 1793. As any farmer knows, a farm requires much heavy work daily. Girls don't do heavy work: they don't plow fields, muck out the stables, or spread the results of the mucking in the fields. They don't even groom the horses, usually. That's all boy work. If the family had no boys, the wretched old fathers with the aching backs did all the heavy work.

That's why there was such a big change in Thomas' life on that June 10, 1797, when Elam came into the world.

Someday, Thomas considered, he might lean his pitchfork against the wall. Maybe just sit on the porch. Smoke his pipe. Doze a little, once in a while, if he felt like it. Farmers dream about things like that. It was their right.

So it was written. Somewhere.

Sure, farmers needed girls. Girls fed the chickens, gathered the eggs. Did the cooking, fixed meals for their brothers so they could grow big and strong and do the heavy work. That's the way it always was. And that's the way it would always be.

It was the order of things.

So it was written. Somewhere.

So it was agreed that the Browns would move, and that they would move to Berkshire County in Massachusetts where Thomas grew up. Elizabeth probably would have preferred to stay in Herkimer County where her friends were and her church was. But she was a woman, and they're not the ones to make the important decisions. Even if she was English. Important decisions were made by the head of the family, and the head of the family was a man. Even if he was Scottish.

So it was written. Somewhere.

So, even before Elam was a year old, the Browns packed up and moved to that glorious place in Massachusetts where rocks didn't grow bigger and heavier.

And it was well that they *had* moved when they did, for after the furniture was all unpacked and the new hen house was built, Elizabeth birthed again. *Another boy!* Elam's little brother, to be named Chauncy, arrived on August 4, 1799.

Thomas considered that they maybe needed a bigger barn. Maybe a bigger pigsty, too. *Maybe a new pipe.*

> *1799, December 14: George Washington died at his home in Mt. Vernon at the age of sixty-seven. The last words in his diary:* "'Tis well."

Indeed, 'twas well in Berkshire County too. Elizabeth found a new church, made new friends. She became happy with her new home and new barn and new pigsty and happy husband. *Even if he* was *a Scot.*

In time, Eliza and Sophronia happily tended to the growing flock of chickens in the new chicken house, happily gathering eggs in such quantity that the extras were sold as surplus. Father Thomas happily farmed and watched the boys grow bigger.

Things were going exactly according to plan.

But things were a'changin,' too.

> *1801, March 4: Thomas Jefferson is inaugurated as the third president of the United States.*

Elizabeth birthed again, on January 18, 1802. *Another son!* Her Scottish husband was most delighted, and hardly able to believe his growing good fortune. *Another* son! *A three son farm!* The possibilities were endless!

1803, January 18: President Jefferson seeks authorization from Congress to explore the "Northwest Territory," choosing his personal secretary Meriwether Lewis to form a "Corps of Discovery" for that purpose.

Thomas was so pleased that he usurped one of Elizabeth's few prerogatives by assuming the privilege of naming the boy himself. Bursting with pride, he acclaimed to the world the perfect name for the new-born son in honor of the newest President of the United States: *Thomas Jefferson Brown!*

It was said that land won by The 1783 Treaty of Paris at the end of the war with Great Britain east of the Mississippi River, called the "Northwest Territory," was virgin; especially in an area called "Ohio.". To Thomas, that meant it would be deeper than the soil in Massachusetts. Richer, too.

Deep, rich soil. Farmers everywhere wanted deep, rich soil. Without rocks. Farmers would come from all over. From Massachusetts or Germany or Ireland. Especially, they would come from Europe, where only the wealthy could afford to buy land. America offered land for anyone that would farm it. And they all yearned to farm in wondrous deep, rich, virgin soil. The finest farmland in all the world.

That first blast from the hypothetical shotgun stirred Thomas' dreams of the relaxed pipe on the porch. But the second blast, just a month later, galvanized him into action.

1803, April 30: The United States purchases the Louisiana territory from France. [Arkansas, Missouri, Iowa, Oklahoma, Kansas, and Nebraska. Also: portions of Minnesota, North Dakota, South Dakota, New Mexico, Texas, Montana, Wyoming, Louisiana, Alberta, and Saskatchewan.]

Thomas' cup runneth over. What to do? Ohio or Louisiana? He was awash in riches. But, which? Either of those places it was said, would be a farmer's dream! And the land…why, the land would be *free.* Or pretty-much free. The country would need farmers to settle, farmers to plow, farmers to seed the land. They had to feed this great new country, didn't they?

What luck, to even *be* here! At this very time and place! Surely, farmers would stream in from everywhere like clouds of locusts, from all over the world, especially places where the soil was worn out from all those centuries of use.

It was time to strike, yet again.

And, just to prove the point, God himself gave him three sons, hadn't he?

He wondered if God had spoken to Elizabeth yet.

He must have. After all: he'd spoken to Moses, hadn't he?

1803, July 4: Lewis chooses William Clark, a former army comrade, to share the command of the Corps of Discovery.

TWO

Ohio

1804-1818

1804, May 14: Lewis & Clark leave St. Charles, Missouri, to explore the Louisiana Purchase and the so-called "Oregon territory" to the Pacific Ocean.

Moses operated a tavern in Lenox, Berkshire County, Massachusetts. No one (but God) would ever dare to call him Moses, however. In Lenox, and especially in the tavern, they called him "The Colonel," with emphasis on **Colonel.** No one seemed to know how he came to be called **The Colonel,** but no one dared to ask, not that they cared very much. It was said that he had won that rank in the Revolutionary War, but many old soldiers called themselves "Colonel" and folks feared to ask to see their credentials.

Moses might have been a real colonel, for he acted like one and spoke with a deep gruff voice like colonels do. A humorless-looking stocky middle-aged fellow with a bit too much weight around the middle, he also *looked* like a colonel. It was a fact that a great many veterans of the Revolutionary War frequented the Colonel's tavern.

A country tavern sold ale for the thirsty and food for the hungry. It also provided room and board for the traveler and a stable for the traveler's horse, all for a price. It goes without saying that, sooner or later, a thirsty veteran with no wherewithal in his pocket would happen by and ask for a cool ale to wet a parched throat. Or a meal for a growling stomach. A room, perhaps. The colonel, being a colonel, most certainly would demand some coin before he even drew the ale. Desperate dickering often led whatever in the veteran's pocket might have value. When the first poor veteran laid a "Bounty Land Warrant" on the bar, the Colonel saw a golden opportunity.

During the Revolutionary War, an impecunious Continental Congress offered bounty land warrants as an inducement to military service: free land in the public domain to those who served, in accordance to rank: from 100 acres for a private to 1,100 aces for a major general. By the end of 1802, about 14,000 warrants had been issued, greatly increasing the odds that many a thirsty veteran might seek surcease in the Colonel's tavern.

In time, the Colonel amassed a considerable number of land warrants, many obtained for much less than actual value. It is said that, at one time, he owned some 8,000 acres of land. But land obtained as an investment has no real value until it is sold. When he discovered that a significant number of his warrants were located in Range 17, Township 4, Section 4 of United States Military Lands in the middle of Ohio, he would have become struck by an epiphany equal to *The Coming of the Magi.*

In accordance with the English characteristic of naming new places after the old, the astute Colonel would call the Ohio settlement "Berkshire," thus making the offer irresistible to any from the rock-bound lands of Massachusetts!

Thomas soon heard of the "New Berkshire," as did every other farmer in the county, and was as intrigued as the rest. But the fast-talking tavern-keeper Byxbe (Moses from time to time changed his name, retaining the rank, possibly because he felt Moses sounded like a charlatan, not to be trusted.) The United States had suddenly grown considerably with the gift of Ohio: President Jefferson was looking even farther afield to the Pacific Ocean by sending Lewis and Clark on their "Voyage of Discovery." Thomas, as a methodical Scot, would have emulated the President taking a ride to Ohio.

And, maybe, even take a look at Byxbe's "Berkshire."

He first broached the subject to Elizabeth and was taken aback by her lack of enthusiasm at the thought of moving again. The house fell silent at the very mention of the word "Ohio." Even the children were quiet. But he was, after all, the "Head of the Household." And the Head of the Household made the family's major decisions.

So it was written. Somewhere.

The Head of the Household eased off: he was, after all, methodical. He might have pretended that the *major decision* was not so important after all. He didn't mention the matter again for a week, and that wasn't until after she, herself, had asked him when he was going to go on his "Corps of Discovery."

1804, June: Lewis & Clark camp beside the Missouri River where the City Hall of Weston, Missouri would one day be built.

Much surprised, he rode off on horseback early the very next day, while her approval was yet at hand. He headed westerly with the morning sun warm on his back until he encountered a vast inland sea, which he knew must be Lake Eire. He kept left, coursing along its southern shore, still heading westerly, following a rough map provided him by Byxbe to the location of the "Military Lands." He soon entered the new State of Ohio: then, after a rather dull ride of several days along the muddy banks of the lake, the shore turned somewhat sharply to the right. He would now be leaving Ohio, but he rode on, knowing he would be approaching Detroit. In that town, he hoped, he might find sleeping accommodation.

Detroit, situated on the strait connecting Lakes Eire and Huron, looked to have several hundred houses in a somewhat dismal location. Several large stone warehouses stood directly on the waterfront, which he assumed must be the reason for the town in the first place, for he saw no other reason for its existence. Nevertheless, he was greatly relieved to find a comfortable-looking tavern near the water that might provide a decent meal and a bed.

On the following morning, not unhappy at the prospect of leaving Detroit behind, he headed back toward Ohio, near what he supposed must be the approximate western boundary of that State. After another quite long ride he arrived at a village called

Cincinnati, which, according to the map, was near Ohio's southwest corner. The town occupied the north bank of the Ohio River in a rather pleasant setting: like Rome and a number of other places, Cincinnati was presumed to be located on seven hills, although Thomas was unable to identify any of them.

In any case, he decided Cincinnati might be conducive to transportation or industry, but not to farming. He had now traversed the northerly and westerly boundaries of Ohio without finding anything better than he already had in Massachusetts. It was well that he had gone on this "Voyage of Discovery," he would have concluded. Now becoming anxious, he felt that Byxbe's Ohio Berkshire would be no better than his own Massachusetts Berkshire. In the morning, he concluded, he would head for home: in a northeasterly direction, right through the center of Ohio, where he hoped to locate that State's new Berkshire.

A cathedral-like forest of immense trees seemed to go on interminably, so thick they blanked out the sun; certainly not a good location for a farm. But after riding for a considerable distance, he came upon a large clearing and welcomed the sun on his back. This was a most beautiful place: slowly, he dismounted, and was surprised by the softness of the soil beneath his feet. He knelt to scoop a handful, finding it moist and black.

Good, rich farmer's soil. The "virgin soil" they talked about.

The Colonel arrived on horseback, but that didn't do much for his image. He still didn't look much like a colonel. He rode slowly toward Thomas and, in true Byxbe fashion, began speaking without a greeting, although this little encounter between neighbors was almost a thousand miles from home.

Thomas rose to his feet and responded in kind, without even a nod.

Like a preacher launching into a sermon without even a preliminary prayer, Byxbe began his sales pitch. He rattled on that the new County Seat might be located here: then, apparently noting that Thomas appeared unimpressed by that information, quickly added that the new State Capitol might even be situated in this very spot!

Of course, such elaboration had only a negative effect on Thomas, who sought farmland, not political land. Although he didn't believe a word of the Colonel's pontificating, he allowed his handful of black soil to dribble back to earth in a show of disinterest.

It appeared that the wily colonel sensed a problem: he backtracked and denied everything. He explained that the story about the state capital was not yet *absolutely* certain, and that it might be many years before the *rumor* could be confirmed. By the time the Colonel had at last concluded his dissertation, even the arrival of the County Seat was in serious doubt.

Upon Thomas's return to Berkshire in Massachusetts, he was presented with a brand new surprise.

Elizabeth was going to have another baby!
Minerva arrived December 9, 1804.

Since Minerva was a daughter, her arrival didn't do much for Thomas' cause. Nevertheless, now confidently entrenched in his commanding "Head of Household" role, he announced that they would be moving to Ohio in the new year.

> *1805: British frigates stop all ships off New York to strip them of seamen supposed by the captain to be British subjects.*

It's a seven hundred mile walk from Berkshire County, Massachusetts to Berkshire County, Ohio. And walk they did, most of those miles. An un-sprung wagon crossing over the Alleghenies can be bouncy and uncomfortable, especially if the wagon is jammed with two adults, five children, a baby, and everything else a family needs to survive, including a very sizeable flock of chickens. Ordinarily, no one would ride in the wagon, because the extra weight would tire the horses sooner. But Elizabeth did ride from time to time, for she needed to cradle six-month-old Minerva on her lap at various times. The chickens, of course, also were permitted the riding privilege at all times, no matter how noisy or indiscriminate they might be.

Elam was, by this time, seven years old. Like any young boy, he thought the long walk was delightful, especially through the woods. How else would one have the freedom, to peer longer at things he might want to peer at? To poke at bugs or lizards that he wanted to poke at? Six-year-old Chauncy peered and poked with him, and together they assisted three-year-old Thomas Jefferson through the muddy patches.

Winding down to Wheeling, then, upon crossing the Ohio River, they were at last in the new State of Ohio. On they went through to a little village called Zanesville with eight to ten cabins and a small mill. Through tiny Newark: only four or five cabins. And to the tiniest place of all: Granville, but a single cabin. At last, over a difficult road just surveyed in by Azariah Root to Mr. Root's cabin.

> *1805, April 29: [Montana] Lewis & Clark estimate that the herd of buffalo they encounter number 10,000 and other game "so plenty and tame that some of the party clubbed them out of their way."*

At last, they found themselves in Berkshire Corners, as the place is now called. Arriving on a gorgeous afternoon in October, all had lasted the journey none the worse for wear except for some ignorant chickens that squawked off into the woods every time their pen door in the bouncing wagon swung open.

The State Capital hadn't arrived. Nor had the County Seat.

Thomas kicked at the good dirt by way of celebration.

They were the proud owners of 150 acres, being Lot 24 of the United States Military Lands, Range 17, Township 4, Section 4, State of Ohio.

April 18, 1806: US Congress passes Non-importation Act to forbid the importation of certain British goods in order to coerce Great Britain to halt the impressment of American sailors.

It became immediately obvious in Berkshire Corners that land sales by the ubiquitous Colonel Byxbe back in Massachusetts were going very well indeed, for new residents arrived weekly. *It might,* Thomas thought, *be a good idea to build a hotel.*

People were building their houses just anywhere, he noted. Even where a new road might go. *It might also be good to create a bit of government. A "Berkshire Township," perhaps.*

Colonel Byxbe, on his way back to Berkshire Corners in the summer, paused for a stopover in Pittsburgh. There he met Judge Henry Baldwin, who enjoyed a prestigious reputation because he had been appointed by President Andrew Jackson, and any judge appointed by the President himself was a force to be reckoned with. It happened, the Colonel learned, that this eminent federal judge also had under his care or possession some 16,000 acres of Ohio land. Some of this was through inheritance from his illustrious half-brother Abraham Baldwin. Other acreage was by assignment, but that didn't matter to Moses Byxbe. Any sort of title to any sort of Ohio land could be parlayed upward.

The parallels between these two must have been astounding even to them. History records that the reputation of the Judge was not always above reproach, nor were his activities always the epitome of decorum.

Moses Byxbe came away from the meeting a changed man: here, he felt, was the best possible partner to have.

When Byxbe arrived back in Berkshire Corners to find Thomas preparing to establish a new Township government, he nearly exploded. Such a folly, he felt, could complicate any devious plans that might be cooked up with his esteemed new partner.

Certainly, it wouldn't be wise to allow a would-be farmer with a wagon load of chickens and children to ruin everything, especially after the trouble with Dr. Lamb.

That doctor, Byxbe noted, looking anxiously around, had not yet arrived to establish his practice. And if the would-be farmer standing before him stirred up some new governments to foil his plans, the doctor might *never* arrive.

> *1806, September 23: Lewis & Clark arrive back in St Louis, bringing from the West great quantities of information on vegetation, animals, Indians, and the geography of the region.*

> *1806, November 14: Zebulon Pike discovers Pike's Peak in Colorado.*

Dr. Reuben Lamb and his wife arrived in Berkshire Corners. The young Doctor, while on the lookout for a suitable place to establish a new practice, had met the Colonel by chance in Pittsburgh just before Byxbe's meeting with Judge Baldwin. It appears that a very serious illness had developed in the Byxbe household, although the "serious illness" has not been defined: nor is it recorded which member of the household was afflicted. It is supposed, however, that the likelihood is great that the member with the problem was the Colonel himself, and that, considering the Colonel's temperament, the problem very well could have been that of high blood pressure.

In any case, Dr. Lamb had come to Berkshire Corners because Colonel Byxbe had assured him the Corners would be a most wonderful place to start a new practice. However, Dr. Lamb had heard of the slow progress of Berkshire (as the new place was sometimes beginning to be called) and had moved instead to Worthington, a new settlement some ten miles farther south. (The Colonel had temporarily suffered a defeat, although he did later convince the doctor that he should return.)

Berkshire did have a new school, built with round logs at the corner of Granville Road, and split logs for the seats and benches. It was in this school that Elam Brown, now ten years old, received his first formal instruction, from a Miss Thompson. It is recorded that here "he first drank from the fountain of knowledge," and that he became interested in history and geography.

From the beginning, the boy cautiously adopted the characteristic of speaking slowly and carefully, even to the point of being taciturn. He discovered that the approach made him appear wise. The trait probably came from his father, who spoke in the same fashion, especially when dealing with people like Moses Bxybe.

1807, June 22: HMS Leopard pours broadsides into USS Chesapeake, rendering her helpless. Leopard's officers then impress members of the American crew.

The good citizens of Berkshire Corners elected Thomas Justice of the Peace in Franklin County. About the same time, the first church services in the village were held in the little Brown cabin. (It was not reported if the results of the election had any effect on the church services.)

1807, November 15: Peter Hardeman Burnett is born at Nashville, Tennessee. He spends his youth in Williamson County, Missouri.

Colonel Byxbe had by now become thoroughly disenchanted with every aspect of Berkshire Corners, and greatly regretted he had encouraged Thomas to move there in the first place. Now, the rapscallion had been elected Justice of the Peace! The Colonel decided it might be wise to divest himself of his holdings in the area, rather than jeopardizing a promising relationship with his new friend Judge Baldwin. He began at once to turn over all his remaining property holdings to his son. Moses Byxbe, Jr. was delighted.

1807, December 22: Embargo Act passed by US Congress against Britain and France to rationalize the plunder of US shipping. (Revoked March 11, 1809)

The Colonel had been aware that a new County was forming in Ohio. In the short period of time since Ohio had been admitted to the Union on March 3, 1803, it had grown so rapidly as to become unwieldy. The *Powers That Be* in Columbus determined that a new, separate County should be formed. (It is not known if Judge Baldwin had a hand in this.) Whatever the political circumstance, on February 10, 1808, the brand new County of Delaware was formed by separating a portion of Franklin County.

Thomas had earlier been opposed to the formation of the new County. Among other reasons for the opposition, he would lose his position as a Franklin County Justice of the Peace simply because that County had gone away. The Byxbes had struck their first blow.

But the elder Byxbe did not yet abandon the battle.

His old friend Azariah Root was to remain in Berkshire Corners, now in Delaware County: Moses was not yet ready to walk away from him. They decided to go together to the State Capital to request funds for the construction of a north/south turnpike right through Berkshire Corners. Furthermore, they planned to ask the Governor to appoint the surveyor Azariah as Road Commissioner to build the turnpike! As if that were not audacious enough, they asked Thomas to go along with them to Columbus, because of his prestige as a former Justice of the Peace.

So they went. And they were granted the funds to build the turnpike

But the Governor didn't appoint Mr. Root to be Road Commissioner. He appointed Thomas Brown.

Both Byxbe and Root must have been beside themselves with fury. History does not record their conversation during the trip back to Berkshire Corners. Nor does it record whether or not they even traveled together.

But the rivalry between the two camps was not yet over. Because of the creation of the new Delaware County, an election became necessary for the post of Major of the newly formed Delaware Battalion Militia. Moses Byxbe, Jr. ran for the position, as did Thomas. Afterward, Moses claimed that he had indeed won, but the claim was hotly disputed by Thomas and his friends. Shouting matches, threats, even loaded guns were brought to the fore. At one point, tensions became so dangerous that Thomas had Moses Junior arrested.

While the charges were being heard, the Governor stepped in and appointed Thomas Brown as Major of the Delaware Battalion.

The matter was laid to rest. Now it was "Major Thomas Brown." As custom would have it, once a military officer, always a military officer. Mr. Thomas Brown had become *Major Thomas Brown,* and he would forever bear that title.

But the problem was *still alive.* Following the dismissal of the charges, father Moses (who, of course, was still the Colonel) ordered a new election.

Which Major Brown lost.

1808, December 8: James Madison elected President of the United States.

Little Elam, now twelve years old, had grown until he could no longer be called "Little Elam," although, much to his everlasting regret, he hadn't quite attained the height he would have preferred. Regardless of his stature, or, perhaps, because of it, he became fascinated by histories citing a goodly number of power figures that suffered from deficiencies of height, but had nevertheless accomplished great things in spite of the handicap: or, indeed, *because* of it. First and foremost was Admiral John Paul Jones, without whom the Americans might still have been toasting the King of England. There was Napoleon Bonaparte. And the Englishman Lord Horatio Nelson, although, as a supremely patriotic American, Elam felt no compulsion to revere. Even if Elam did have some English in his lineage.

> *1809, February 12: Abraham Lincoln is born on the Sinking Spring Farm near Hodgenville, Kentucky. October 11: Lewis Merriwether, of Lewis & Clark fame, died near Nashville, Tennessee.*

> *1810: John Jacob Astor of the American Fur Company outfits "The Astor Expedition" to search for a trail to the Pacific. The result becomes known as "The Oregon Trail."*

A new, larger school of squared logs replaced the original round-log structure built by Colonel Byxbe east of the corners on the Granville Road. The new school, taught by Miss Thompson from Worthington, served ten scholars, Elam Brown among them. It was here that it was said "he drank from the fountain of knowledge as found in books and laid the foundation for that love of literature which he has found in after years so beneficial."

> *1810, September 16: The Mexican War of Independence begins when a priest named Miguel Hidalgo y Costilla seizes control of the local militia in San Miguel.*

Major Thomas Brown built the first brick house in Berkshire Township on his property, replacing the round-log cabin that had served so well. A little north of the corners, on the right hand side of North Galena Road, it was a large multi-gabled two story house, plus a sizeable attic. The house sported embrasures in the upper outside walls which could be used as gun slits should the settlement come under attack.

The Major began operating a hotel and tavern at the house to service the influx of emigrants to Ohio. The charge for room and board was $1.50 per week if the room was located on the first or second floor: attic rooms were billed at $1.00 per week. Single meals cost fifteen to twenty cents.

The house, a substantial landmark in the area, also served as a rallying point during any real or perceived crises. It also functioned as a church: the Pioneers of this place were a religious people: among them were those of the Episcopalian, Presbyterian, and Methodist beliefs. Their creed adhered to that principle set forth in the Ordinance of 1787: "Religion, morality and knowledge being necessary to good government and the happiness of mankind, schools and the means of education shall forever be encouraged."

> *1811, February 2: Fort Ross settled on the Pacific Coast by the Russians to establish a territorial claim and an agricultural base to serve their northerly settlements.*

> *1811, March: John Jacob Astor establishes Fort Astoria, the first European settlement in Oregon, at the mouth of the Columbia River.*

> *1811: July 9: Surveyor David Thompson posts a claim to the "Oregon Country" on behalf of Great Britain.*

Another little girl was born to Elizabeth on May 12, 1812. The arrival of Delia elevated the total number of girls to four. It is possible, but not recorded, that Major Thomas Brown determined at that point that, as a practical matter, logic might dictate a greater emphasis be placed on operation of a hotel and a lessor one on the plowing of fields, for there were but three boys.

> *1812, June 18: President Madison signs a Declaration of War on the United Kingdom. This is the first time the United States declared war on another nation. Elam might have noted with*

some satisfaction that President Madison stood only five feet, four inches tall and weighed fewer than a hundred pounds.

The "Second War of Independence," as it was generally recognized in its beginning, came slowly to the residents of Berkshire Corners. At the time, they were more concerned about the possibility of attack by the Indians, who were close at hand, than they were by the British who, after all, still lived in far-away England.

Or so these Pioneers thought.

Of course, they had been long aware of the problem with the English impressment of American sailors. Yet, how could the English be separated among them? The language, the dialects, the accents were all the same. It must be conceded that the English ship captains treated their sailors more cruelly than the American captains, and that quite a number had altered their allegiance, given half the chance. But those ships sailed on the oceans, and those oceans were far removed from the borders of Ohio. Let alone, the borders of Berkshire Corners.

The Great American Lakes were closer, however. And Lake Eire actually bordered on Ohio. When it was reported that, on August 16, 1812, the United States had surrendered Detroit to the United Kingdom, the folks in Berkshire sat up and took notice. That was getting *close*. Major Brown was pleased to recall that, at one time, while looking for a place to settle, he had sensibly decided not to settle in Detroit.

In only a very few days after the loss of Detroit, the upstart Americans themselves struck a telling blow. That the blow was against the most powerful Navy in the world made it even more telling.

> *1812, August 19: The* USS Constitution *sinks the British frigate* HMS Guerriere, *in which battle* Constitution *wins the nickname* Old Ironsides.

Now, maybe the *English* would sit up to take notice.

Signs of martial activity begin to emerge even in Berkshire Corners. Captain Aaron Strong's company of militia was activated, requiring the services of former Major Brown as a private, then a corporal from October 7 through December 15, 1812.

> *1813, March 4: James Madison re-elected President of the United States.*

Major Brown served as a sergeant in Captain Ichabod Plumb's Company, 2nd Regiment from May 4 through May 27.

And was a corporal in Kendall's Cavalry from July 26 through August 28.

> *1813, September 10: US Commodore Perry wins Detroit back from UK Commander Barclay in the Battle of Lake Eire, afterward proclaiming "We have met the enemy, and they are ours."*

1814, August 24: British officers eat a dinner at the President's House that had been prepared for President and Mrs. Madison, afterwards setting fire to the house. Americans are outraged.

1814, August 25: Francis Scott Key writes the lyrics for The Star Spangled Banner at the Battle of Fort McHenry, Maryland.

1814, December 24: The War of 1812 ends with the Treaty of Ghent.

1815, January 8: Andrew Jackson, aided by the pirate Jean Lafitte, and unaware that the war had already ended by virtue of the Treaty of Ghent, defeats the British in the Battle of New Orleans.

The war at last was over. Berkshire Corners began to relax.

Major Brown's hotel thrived: more and more emigrants poured in to Ohio. So thankful was he that on Sunday mornings, the big room that normally served as the restaurant and tavern was utilized for church services.

Well suited for such services, the room had numerous dining tables, each surrounded by four benches, permitting additional seating whenever the room exceeded its usual maximum, which happened frequently. The preacher usually orated to his flock while standing atop a bench in the corner of the room, allowing him to be more clearly heard.

Locating preachers was never a problem. There always seemed to be preachers, perhaps ordained and perhaps not, that floated through communities such as Berkshire Corners on Sunday mornings, ready and able to flog a willing congregation, to be rewarded with an ample breakfast, courtesy of the house, and a hatful of coin. Preachers and would-be preachers, it seemed, typically wore commodious hats which not only served to protect them from the weather but, to the casual observer, also looked to be nearly empty of coin when the preacher looked most poor and pious at the end of the service.

Of course, it should also be noted that the tavern's canny proprietor doubtlessly noted that, having filled the room on Sundays (and all other religious holidays, of course) the congregants usually lingered afterwards to eat, drink, and ostensibly discuss whatever ecclesiastical subjects the preacher might have touched upon.

Religious or business advantages notwithstanding, Elam had begun to more strongly dislike the gradual shifting of interest from the farm. Increasingly, he found himself repelled by the strong odor of liquor that emanated not only from the liquor itself, but from the room, even when empty: as if the rough walls themselves had so absorbed the odor that the tavern reeked of it, even the first thing in the morning.

The once-grand fields of grain that once surrounded the house had been reduced to a vegetable patch, capable only to provide a few fresh items for the hotel's kitchen. Elam longed for the open air, the intoxicating odor of good moist earth.

He was a farmer.

Not a tavern-keeper.

And his father noticed. One day, he confronted Elam with the question, and Elam flatly confirmed the truth. The Major understood, for he had been suffering from the very same anxieties himself. He lay a hard major's hand on Elam's shoulder and proclaimed that Elam must go right ahead and do that which he felt he had to do. He didn't mention that he had once done the same himself.

But there was a caveat. The Major added that he must wait until he had "Come of Age."

Elam nodded in agreement, although he didn't know what "Come of Age" meant.

1816, July 25: Major Thomas Brown, 47, died at his home in Berkshire Corners, Ohio.

Everything changed when the Major died. Elam's life had suddenly become forfeit: as oldest son, he had become the head of the family!

The agreement with the Major, he felt, had died with the Major. Elam resolved that he would not abandon his mother and the rest of the family. His life had become forfeit. But that was a problem he could put behind him. More important problems were at hand.

Like serving as *head of the family.*

They installed the Major in an empty bedroom on the first floor of the hotel, to lie in State for a few days.

It appeared that, although he had been such a revered and respected citizen in Berkshire since his arrival some twelve years earlier, his death nevertheless caused little of a stir. Many did come to pay homage and a few lingered in the tavern over a glass of ale, but none lingered overlong, which was not surprising. No one intended irreverence, but most in attendance were farmers, and it is right that a farmer must not stay away from his farm overlong.

Just as the farms' cows needed regular milking, so did the hotel need daily, if not hourly, maintenance. Life must go on: the guests must be attended to, funeral or no funeral. Diners sought their food: drinkers their drink. And so it also was for the horses in the stables.

It must be said that the hotel was well-run. Sister Eliza, now twenty-six years old, had assumed most of the day-to-day operations. Sophronia, 23, served as Eliza's principal assistant, handling the bookkeeping. That responsibility perfectly suited her at the moment, for her ultimate goal was to teach in the Berkshire school.

Younger brother Chauncy, seventeen, led the horses of the arriving guests to the stables. That stinking place had become his major responsibility. Because, for the sake of convenience, it was located so near to the hotel, it required the unwelcome necessity of shoveling out manure and transporting same by wheelbarrow to the vegetable patch.

Every successful hotel has a flamboyant clerk at the desk to greet incoming guests with broad smiles, and that would be Thomas Jefferson. Only fourteen, he acted most graciously, always accompanying the broad smile with deep bows.

The chief responsibility for Minerva, at age twelve, was to look after her four-year-old sister. Little Delia was not big, nor was she a big problem: most of the time, Minerva also helped out in the kitchen to allow her mother more time to work the stove.

But all paused on July 28, 1816, when they simply closed the hotel for the day, to lay the Major to his final rest in the Berkshire Cemetery.

When the ceremony had finished, they all went back to the hotel. Elam's mother took her son aside to tell him that the Major had told her about the pact between them.

He was free to go.

He had at last "Come of Age."

> *1816, December 31: Reconstruction of the President's House is considered complete, now that the walls have been painted white to cover the black marks made by the fire.*

The hotel, the restaurant, the tavern, all prospered. Even the stables had prospered. Even the vegetable garden prospered.

It was the vegetable garden that had become Elam's principal responsibility: after, of course, being *head of family.* The vegetable garden was the remaining vestige of the Major's once grand fields of wheat, and the only portion of the holdings in which Elam had much interest. He was, he felt, a farmer, and had little interest in the functions of the hotel.

But his desire to see the West flared. He devoured any information he could accumulate, pinned the few available maps to the walls of his room. He bored the family near to death when the evening farm chores had finished, the dishes washed and shelved, the wood brought indoors and stacked by the stove for morning. His mother would see he was slipping from the nest, anxious to test his wings. He realized that when at last the fateful day arrived and he blurted out his intentions, she would dissolve with all those bottled-up tears, as mothers do. At the end, he was sure, she would cave in, as mothers ultimately must.

Brothers Chauncy and Thomas by this time had grown weary of the increasingly delicate discussions and would absolutely, wholeheartedly and unreservedly resolved that they could most adequately farm the vegetable patch without older brother Elam.

Day to day, Elam became more and more restless. The combination of his curiosity, the wanderlust inherited from his father, and *his* father, the tantalizing reports of Lewis and Clark and the imaginations of mighty rivers (they had no such rivers in the East) and snowy mountains (nor snowy mountains) tore away his interest from those confounded soft and gentle hills of Ohio. He dreamed of high jagged mountains, snow on their tops. Others did, too, a great many others, coming by the shipload from that vaunted "Old World." A veritable people tidal wave churned across the oceans, and even from the American states, as anxious as he was to see those places where the thousands of buffaloes still roamed.

Fortunately, he *did* have an ally in his friend Charles Gregory. Charles appeared to be older than

Elam, for he was taller and more heavily built than his friend, although two years younger. Charles had come to Ohio as a child, as had Elam. They had much in common, frequently walking together, talking of those far off lands with the buffalo and the Indians, thrilling with the simple words "Out West." Someday, they promised themselves, they'd go there.

It was time for the "Come of Age. The day declared by the Major that the boy had become a man, free to go. Elam was ready.

He had talked with his friend about the day many times, and it was fully acknowledged between them that they would part on that day, never to see each other again. When it at last arrived, he hugged his brothers, saving the bigger hugs for his sisters. Lastly, the biggest of all for his mother. They hung together and fought the sobs, no matter how many times they had promised they would be above that. Sharply then, before the wrenching goodbyes grew to the melting point, Elam flung over his shoulder the flour sack packed with just a few meager belongings. Down the path he raced, tears blurring his vision. He stumbled over those first steps of the five hundred mile walk to St. Louis. *That place on the very edge of the new frontier, where the rivers were swift and the mountains high.*

St. Louis, he consoled himself, was closer to Ohio than Ohio was to Massachusetts. He had done that walk as a child. The walk to the west wouldn't be so bad at all.

Charles was at Elam's elbow before his friend had gone a mile, striding along with great steps and head bent over like a hulking buffalo. Elam grinned at him, not at all surprised: they were fast friends that understood each other.

Charles had a plan, to which Elam readily agreed, for Charles was that kind of friend. They would hike southwesterly to Cincinnati to the Ohio River. There, they would take a boat down-river to the West. Elam wouldn't ask how Charles happened to have such a plan. *They were friends, after all.*

And it worked. When they reached the river, God *or an angel* had put a sadly dilapidated and derelict canoe in a bed of rushes, barely afloat. Paddles were fashioned with geat speed from similarly derelict flotsam, and they rode haphazardly, one of them bailing constantly while the other paddled all the way to Shawneetown, where they set the canoe free to delight others.

They learned that a road led northwesterly from Shawneetown through Illinois to Woods River, very near St. Louis. Called the Goshen Road because it led to Goshen Settlement, so named by a Baptist minister because he determined it looked like the Biblical Land of Goshen, the road was becoming popular with early settlers looking for a good way to the West. And it was popular to Charles and Elam.

> *1818, October 20: Treaty of 1818 establishes joint control of the "Oregon Country" between the United States and Great Britain for ten years.*

> *1818, December 3: State of Illinois admitted to the Union.*

THREE

Missouri

1818-1819

St. Louis was remarkable. Just fourteen years after Lewis and Clark had returned from the vast western unknown, the place already had a population of four thousand. There must have been five hundred buildings, many of stone: including forty stores, three banks, two distilleries and a brewery. "It looked like a seaport town," someone observed. "Barges and keel boats with masts, sails and rigging line the shore for a mile and a half."

Elam was impressed and disappointed at the same time. Impressed by the size and scope of the place; disappointed because he had thought he'd be in the wilderness here. He had left Charles on the other side of the river in Illinois. Charles had loved it there: as if he'd found Goshen. And, indeed he had. The Land of Goshen was steeped in luxuriant vegetation, just as the Bible said it would be. But Elam was looking for the edge of civilization, and hadn't found it yet, even if he'd spent a good part of his last dollar to get across the Mississippi in a filthy rowboat almost as derelict as the canoe they'd paddled down the Ohio.

The trip from Berkshire had taken almost a month. His boots were worn thin on the soles, his feet sore. Desperately in need of a bath, exhausted, hungry, and near penniless, he decided that leaving Ohio and coming to St. Louis might have been the greatest mistake he had ever made or ever would make.

Nevertheless. at the very moment of his deepest despair, God saw fit to send down an angel, as He is often wont to do. If Sylvester Paddy hadn't happened along on that sticky hot day in October 1818, Elam might have walked all the way back to Ohio, as impossible as that might be. But he had been considering it.

Mr. Paddy, a hearty archetypal red-faced Irishman with a perennial smile and a cheerful word for all was just the medicine Elam needed. Lumber from the new Paddy sawmill on the Big Piney River, he explained with his booming voice and waving of knobby hands, was to be floated north down the Gasconade River (wherever that was) to the Missouri River, then east on the Missouri to the Mississippi, then south on that mighty river the remaining eighteen miles to St. Louis.

Elam had no idea why it was necessary to go to so much trouble to get lumber for a town already built of stone. But Mr. Paddy offered employment as a rafter, to be paid the princely sum of $1.50 per hour. The tired, dirty, starving derelict set his doubts aside.

Lumber rafting, it turned out, wasn't quite as idyllic as it sounded. It was brutally hard work manning the long sweep oars at either end of the lumber rafts. If they grounded on sandbars or drifted ashore at turns in the various rivers, which they often did, it became necessary to heave the ponderous steering oars in directions they hadn't wanted to go. Such heaving was always accompanied by much shouting and swearing by his burly raft-mates, who failed to see why such a skinny little fellow as this should even want to work on such a manly object as a lumber raft in the first place.

> *1818, October 20: The United States and Great Britain fix the boundary of the two nations at the 49th parallel between Lake of the Woods and the crest of the Rocky Mountains. No boundary was decided upon farther west. Oregon was declared open territory for ten years.*

It was difficult not to doubt the wisdom of this newly-chosen career. Elam was, after all, a farmer, and farmers typically did not choose to play about on rafts in muddy rivers. However, he now bathed more frequently (usually in the rivers), had sufficient income to purchase new trousers, a new pair of boots, and had a bit of coin jingling in his pouch. Nevertheless, on one fine day in March, 1819, he most graciously thanked the ebullient Mr. Paddy for his benevolence, threw the worn flour sack back over his shoulder and headed east across the Mississippi to the brand-new State of Illinois.

Dressed up in his fine new boots and trousers, he thought he'd go look up Charles. See if he had found Goshen yet.

FOUR

Illinois

Madison County

1819-1836

The farmer in Elam had noted the tempting Illinois farms on the walk up the Goshen Road from Shawneetown. Still, the decision to move easterly instead of westerly was difficult, for his aim was to go to the west. Amazed at how quickly it seemed that things had turned around, the farming scene no longer seemed as lush as it had earlier. He was aware that the economy had soured. While rafting the lumber, he had been blissfully unaware of a major financial crisis in the country, subsequently named "The Panic of 1819." The young United States had struggled to pay for two wars. Two of the three banks in St. Louis closed their doors. The value of farmland had plummeted. Many farmers found themselves with more land than they could work and they couldn't afford to hire help.

As it turned out, the "Panic" benefitted him, albeit temporarily. While walking through the new County of Madison, some twenty-five miles east of St. Louis, he decided he should be on the lookout for Charles. He asked of any farmers he saw in a field, or anyone he encountered while walking along the roads. In time, he did come upon an itinerant-looking fellow, who recalled a new, young, tall arrival to the area, and pointed down the road to a farm.

The farm did indeed belong to Charles. His old friend greeted him most joyfully, then lamented that the farm was too big, more than he could handle. Elam at once offered to "share-crop" with him, a method of hiring help without the need to pay wages, a system then becoming common in the area. Charles accepted the proposition at once.

Elam now had a roof over his head and a place at a table, and was content. He wrote his family back in Berkshire, describing the canoe ride down the Ohio, the long walk to Woods River, the lumber rafts, and the searching out of Charles Gregory. He posted the letter, fully understanding that, with the unreliability of the embryotic postal system, it might never arrive.

But it did.

Before long, his younger brother Chauncey showed up.

Elam had been plowing a field near the road on one especially warm day, when a familiar *halleo!* caused him to look up. He was so taken aback by the sight of his younger brother that, for a moment, he thought he was back in Berkshire. But it was a very short moment: almost immediately, their arms were about each other. The ox pulling the plow, contentedly unperturbed by the excitement of the hugging, continued with the more practical business of plowing.

Elam hurried after the slowly departing plow, although it was hardly necessary to hurry. He shouted questions over his shoulder to his brother, who therefore must hurry through the freshly turned earth after him. Charles, working on the other side of the field, heard the shouting, and wondered what the ruckus was all about. The ruckus intensified when he recognized his Berkshire friend.

Chauncey explained that Elam's letter had indeed been received. All in the family had read the letter, again and again. They had laughed together about his tale of the decrepit canoe, the homemade paddles. And Chauncey had become hooked. He simply *had* to follow.

Mother had at last given her permission. He had left at once, following Elam's path: the walk to Cincinnati, the ride down the Ohio. He couldn't find any old canoes lying around, but a friendly keel-boatman gave him a ride downstream. Debarking at Shawneetown, he then followed the well-traveled Goshen Road to Woods River.

In time, with both Elam and Chauncey pitching in, Charles' farm had begun to prosper. The three of them were even able to find the time to serve in *The Mounted Rangers,* a militia group formed to combat so-called Indian depredations, although they were unsuccessful in finding any Indians that had depredated.

One day, Elam learned that Congress had reduced to eighty acres the size of a tract of land that one could buy for $1.25 per acre. That meant the eighty acres could be purchased for a measly one hundred dollars! The problem was that he didn't have a hundred dollars. But he had more than fifty dollars. And when he asked Chauncey, he found his brother had even more than that. They stared thoughtfully at each other for a moment, but the result of their thinking was a foregone conclusion.

*1820, December 6: James Monroe is re-
elected President of the United States.*

Apple Creek, Illinois
1821-1824

And so it was that, on June 27, 1821, the Brown
brothers, Elam and Chauncey, jointly purchased the
eighty acres described as the West ½ of Section 11,
Township 11 North, Range 12 West, 3rd Principal Base
& Meridian, located near the hamlet of Apple Creek.
(Today Whitehall Township, Greene County, Illinois.)

As it turned out, Elam's good fortune didn't end
with that happy purchase some forty miles north of the
Charles Gregory farm. Unbeknownst to them at the
time, one Thomas Allen, also from Madison County,
had six months earlier purchased the Northeast ¼ of
Section 22,Township 11 North, Range 12 West, 3rd
Principal Base & Meridian, only a mile from the
property just purchased by the two Browns. And, as
luck would have it, Thomas Allen had an attractive
daughter named Sarah.

*1821, August 10: Missouri admitted to
the Union.*

Elam was a very shy fellow, especially whenever
he had found himself among girls close to his own age.
On those rare occasions, he literally choked up and
avoided eye contact by a careful study of his boots, as
if to assure himself that he hadn't stepped in something
he shouldn't have. The subject girl, upon observing

such a display of shyness, typically smiled compassionately, making matters worse.

However, his very first encounter with Sarah was different. Words flowed immediately, and without ceasing. The conversation, of course, had been started by Sarah; later, Elam had absolutely no idea what the subject was. He only realized that, for the very first time in his life, he was able to talk to a girl and didn't want to stop.

1821, August 24: Treaty of Cordoba establishes Mexico's independence from Spain. The new Republic grants lands in Texas state on the condition settlers convert to Catholicism and assume Mexican citizenship to stop possible expansion by the United States.

Elam was smitten. From that very first moment, he knew he would to marry her. But, given his methodical nature and his thoughtful manner of speech, he dawdled for nearly a year before he worked up the courage to ask *her*. Following a positive reply to the first question, he braced himself for the far more dangerous process of asking Mr. Allen for her hand. That turned out to be much easier than he had supposed. Her father, in true farmer fashion, was already aware that he had more daughters than he really needed to collect the eggs in the henhouse: in good father-in-law fashion, he probably slapped Elam on the back and wanted to know what had taken him so long. Elam and Sarah married in the Apple Creek

Church on January 10, 1823. Chauncey Brown, the Best Man, wore his best overalls to the ceremony.

> *1823, February 28: Supreme Court rules on Johnson v. M'Intosh, laying the foundation for landownership in the United States, asserting that the purchase of Louisiana from France did not include the rights of the tribes who inhabited the area.*

The three of them: Elam, Sarah, and Chauncey lived happily in the small house they built at Apple Creek. On October 16, 1823, Sarah gave birth to her first-born son. Everything changed.

She named the boy Thomas Allen in honor of her father, but that was not the problem. The problem was that, very suddenly, four people now inhabited the small house. One of those people, although very small, proved to be exceedingly noisy at inopportune times. The house became smaller very quickly: with the approach of an Illinois winter, it would become yet smaller. Chauncey never complained about the baby, but a growing discomfiture had become apparent. In addition, there would be little privacy, which could generate a hardship for two newly-weds so enamored of each other, even if one of them had started out to be very shy. Elam began to search out a different arrangement.

He found it. In early 1824, when he informed Chauncey that his family was about to move, his brother cheerily handed over the $50.00 Elam had provided for his share of the Apple Creek property.

1824, August 15: By invitation of President James Monroe, the Marquis de Lafayette arrives at Staten Island, New York to an artillery salute in his honor upon the nation's fiftieth anniversary.

Morgan County, Illinois
1824-1836

And so it was that the Elam Browns, all three of them, moved some twenty miles north to Morgan County, and purchased the East ½ of the Southwest ¼ of Section 21, Township 15 North, Range 12 West, 3rd Principal Base & Meridian. Happily, the cost was $50.00. They made the trip in style, riding in Elam's new wagon, pulled by the new team of horses. The wagon and the team, he must have thought, was a considerable improvement over a flour sack on his shoulder.

1824, October 17: Lafayette visits George Washington's tomb at Mt. Vernon.

1824, November 4: Lafayette visits Thomas Jefferson at Montecello.

1825, May 8: Lafayette visits Shawneetown, Illinois.

1825, September 6: Lafayette celebrates his 68th birthday party at the White

*House, at the invitation of President
John Quincy Adams.*

The family continued to grow with the birth of a
second son: Warren, on June 19, 1826. Elam found
that he might be facing disaster. After having spent
most of his wherewithal to buy the wagon and horses,
the farm, then to build the house, the pocketbook had
grown more slowly than the family. Another mouth to
feed, however small, would additionally increase the
burden. The ends were no longer meeting, no matter
how hard he worked.

He wasn't alone. A similar hardship was, at that
time, facing other farmers in the area. Farmers who,
when things got tough, went up north to a place called
"Wisconsin" (in Lafayette County), where a person
could dig lead ore right from the surface of the soil.
The only tools needed would be a shovel and a bucket.

Elam grabbed his shovel and a bucket and was off.

*1826, July 4: Thomas Jefferson dies at
Charlottesville, Virginia.*

The lead mining, if scooping dirt from the surface
with a shovel could be called that, proved to be fairly
lucrative. It certainly paid better than raising cattle,
which hardly paid at all. But the "leading," which the
miners (diggers) called it, was very much seasonal
work: upon the approach of winter, the ground grew
too hard to dig. When snow covered the frozen ground,
Elam fled south to his warm house and family in
Illinois.

> *1826, Fall: Peter Burnett returns to Tennessee, settling at Bolivar, Hardeman County, where he works as a hotel clerk.*

> *1826, November 6: Captain F. W. Beechey sails HMS Blossom into San Francisco Bay, noting that a hazardous submerged obstruction (Blossom Rock) may be avoided by aligning the northerly tip of Yerba Buena Island with two large trees (Redwoods) atop the East Bay hills.*

He returned to the diggings in the Spring of 1827. Things had changed: the Winnebago Indian Tribe had begun to show signs of restlessness. Young braves took to watching the miners dig during the day, always keeping their distance, but exuding a hostility that could be felt. In the night, objects began to disappear: hammers, chisels, trousers. The miners took to sleeping with their shovels.

> *1827, August 6: The United States and Great Britain sign a treaty to extend an 1818 agreement to continue joint occupation of Oregon Country.*

They called it "mining," and that could probably be construed as correct. But it was done with a shovel and a bucket: to Elam, it just sounded like "digging." *Badger Holes,* they were called by some, *Lead Mines,* by others. Elam had his own name: *Back Breakers.* He

was thirty years old now, and had grown to hate the
need to do such digging for a living. He was a farmer,
after all. Farmers had to dig for a living, too. *But it was
good digging.* When the first cold winds of October
started, he went home and never came back

> *1827-28: Peter Burnett works in a
> country store. Purchases the store in the
> Spring of 1828.*

Then came a long dry period, with much less rain
than was normal. The family grew better than the
crops: first daughter Margeline arrived April 12, 1829.
Another mouth to feed.

> *1830: Peter Burnett, in serious
> financial trouble, is forced out of
> business. Peter Cooper builds the "Tom
> Thumb," the first steam locomotive in
> America.*

> *1830, July 15: Treaty of Prairie du
> Chien...The said Tribes cede and
> relinquish to the United States forever
> all their right and title to the lands lying
> within the following boundaries, to
> wit...to the Missouri River, thence down
> said Missouri River to the Missouri
> state line...to be assigned and allotted
> under the direction of the President of
> the United States, to the Tribes now
> living thereon, or to other such Tribes...*

Without the income from the lead mining, things were really getting tough. In order to supplement his meager income, on August 1, 1831, Elam proposed himself as a candidate for Justice of the Peace in Morgan County. To his very great surprise, he was accepted, and was commissioned on September 10, 1831 in Walnut Creek, Illinois. Although the pay was meager, he hoped the slight income, combined with the occasional sale of a few calves from their growing herd would see them through.

It got worse. The nation-wide Panic and Depression of 1832 struck Illinois with the unforgiving force of the wintry winds. Demand for beef dissolved: the Brown family hunkered down in their warm house, surviving on meat from the herd and copious quantities of potatoes stored in the pantry which had thoughtfully been planted and nurtured by Sarah through the long dry summer. A new worry was the cholera epidemic that had broken out in New York in the summer of 1832, killing many thousands. The Browns might have been thankful for the whistling eastward winds.

> *1832: Peter Burnett returns to Missouri, $700 in debt, 62 ½ cents in his pocket. He undertakes the study of law. After 15 months of study, he is admitted to the bar.*
> *Abraham Lincoln moves to New Salem, Illinois. He serves as County Surveyor and decides to become a lawyer by teaching himself.*

During that cold, desperate winter, on January 13, 1833, the family grew yet again with the birth of a son into this difficult world.

Sarah named him Lawrence.

> *1833, August 17, 1833: The Congress of Mexico passes An Act for the Secularization of the Missions of California.*

> *1833, October 20: Mountain Man Joseph Walker, on a fur-trapping foray into Alta California, becomes the first Caucasian to look down into the valley that would be named Yosemite.*

> *1833, October 30: Joseph Walker becomes the first Caucasian to observe "trees of the red-wood species, incredibly large—some of which would measure from sixteen to eighteen fathom (108 feet) round the trunk and at the height of a man's head from the ground." (Probably, the Merced Grove of giant sequoias.)*

> *1834, May 20: General Lafayette dies at age 76. Buried in Picpus Cemetery in Paris, he lies under soil from George Washington's grave at Mount Vernon. President Andrew Jackson ordered military posts and ships to fire 24-gun salutes, each shot for a state, flags to fly*

at half-mast for thirty-five days, military officers to wear crepe.

1834: Peter Burnett joins a mercantile partnership.
Abraham Lincoln wins election to the Illinois State Legislature.

1834, August 1: Governor Jose Figueroa grants Rancho Acalanes (3,329 acres) [Contra Costa County, California] to Candelario Valencia, a soldier in the San Francisco Company.

1834: Mexican government secularizes missions and begins to sell or lease mission properties to private citizens.

Somehow, the Browns managed to scrape through until Elam's term as Justice of the Peace expired in 1835, which would end the extra income that had kept them going. At once, Elam ran for another term. Much to his delight, and with heaps of thanks to the greater power above, he was re-elected to a second four-year term!

1835, October 2: Texans revolt against Mexico.

It would have appeared that things couldn't get worse. But then the Depression of 1836 struck and was worse than the Panic and Depression four years earlier.

1836, March 2: Texas declares itself an independent republic. The US is unwilling to recognize The Republic of Texas.

1836, March 6: The Alamo, a fortified mission at San Antonio, Texas, is captured by General Antonio Lopez de Santa Anna. Every Texan was killed except a mother, a child, and a servant.

1836, April 26: Battle of San Jacinto. Santa Anna is captured and forced to sign the Treaties of Velasco, in which he agrees to withdraw from Texan soil and recognize Texan independence.

1836, June 7: William Clark persuades the Indians to sell two million acres to the United States for payment of $7,500 and an agreement to build houses for them on a new reservation west of the Missouri River... Abraham Lincoln moves to Springfield, Illinois, and is admitted to the bar.

The talk was rampant in Morgan County about the so-called proposed "Platte Purchase." in Missouri. Not actually *in* Missouri, but *next* to Missouri. Missouri's western boundary, a straight line top to bottom, would change with the addition of a triangular shaped area westerly to the Missouri River. That triangle, reserved for the Indians by the Treaty of 1830, had been inundated by emigrants seeking the fine farmland it contained. The United States, powerless to stop the emigrants, bought the piece back and sent the Indians across the river.

Elam recalled his days in Missouri, some eighteen years earlier. He had been a young man then: now, he was thirty-nine years old. He'd gone from river-rafting lumber to share-cropping to farming to lead mining. He had made some money and he'd lost some. After eighteen years of struggling, all he had was a worthless farm, a wagon, a team of horses, a herd of skinny cattle and a family to feed.

He broached the subject one evening while they all sat around the supper table. He told all that he had learned about "The Platte," how the land was so rich and fertile. And free, so everyone said. About the emigrants rushing in, even from Europe, to settle. How important it was to be there before all the best parts were taken, especially the bottom lands down by the river. That the Mississippi was so low that year because of the dry summer. How they could swim the cattle across. And the wagon. They'd leave this farm. Just walk away.

The room fell all quiet when he had finished. He sat back in his chair, folded his hands together, and peered into the eyes of his family, one by one: Thomas, Warren, Margeline, even little Lawrence. They all peered back. Except Sarah. She looked away.

Sarah didn't speak.

They talked. Or, rather, Elam did. He talked about the value of bottom land. That rich, black soil created through the centuries by periodic flooding of the river. None better in the world. And free for the asking, they said. He didn't know how that could be, but it was what they all said. It was what he wanted to believe. So he believed.

Normally a cautious man, he always had been wary of anything free. But these were desperate times. And he desperately wanted concurrence from Sarah. He fell silent and waited.

She spoke, so softly that he hardly heard. But he had heard, and he understood. She had said but one word, a single frightening word: *Miasma.*

> *First century, Vitruvius: "For when the morning breezes blow...if they bring with them mist from marshes...the poisonous breath of creatures...they will make the site unhealthy."*

Elam shuddered. In the Deep South, the fearsome-sounding word *Miasma* described poisonous vapors from fetid low places in the earth such as swamps and ponds.

He might have countered by saying that The Platte contained only the Missouri, a very large river without stagnant pools and noxious vapors. It would have had no impact whatsoever on her concern, and it should not have had: during that same period, both the Thames in London and the Seine in Paris were credited with contributing largely to catastrophic outbreaks of Cholera.

But he must have realized he would never convince her: nothing was to be gained by arguing the point further. It was time to go, while he had yet a little coin in his pocket. He stalked down to the County offices and submitted his resignation as Justice of the Peace, sealing the deal. *Now they had only the coin in his pocket.*

There was one more thing he hadn't yet said to Sarah. There would be no point in trying to sell the farm. With the nation in such a great recession, and with Morgan County smack in the middle of it, there wouldn't be any buyers.

They would just hope they'd find some of that good bottom land in the Platte.

Free bottom land.

1836, February 4: John Marsh appears before the ayuntamiento at the Pueblo of Our Lady, the Queen of the Angels (Los Angeles), presents his Harvard B.A. degree, written in Latin, and requests a license to practice medicine. Referred to the Mission San Gabriel for translation, the diploma was found to be correct. John Marsh officially had became a licensed doctor.

FIVE

The Platte

1836-1843

It was a long pull from Morgan County to the Platte. Although the way was long, the actual going wasn't all that bad: the grade alongside the Missouri was quite flat, with plenty of grass for the stock. The good wide trail on the northerly side of the River was packed down hard, probably because so many feet had already gone this way. Elam found himself worrying about all those feet. Would there be any land left in the Platte that hadn't already been taken? He sped up just a wee bit and wished he had a fast boat.

> *Thirty years earlier, Lewis & Clark had paddled up this very same river. In a boat, Elam smiled to himself, thinking that if the Brown family were to go in a boat, it'd have to be something like Noah's Ark. Had it really been thirty years already?*

Elam set a rapid pace, marching out ahead as spritely as he could, at the head of the cattle herd. They lumbered along very well recognizing him as the leader of their flock, as cattle tend to think. A flock, not a herd, for they thought of themselves as members of the choir. Like most choir members, they obediently followed their preacher, the rare objections muted down to grunts so softly spoken so as not to disturb any heavy thoughts or prayers. They did, however, need to be mindful of the fine willow whips wielded by the ushers, Thomas and Warren, who strove to keep the march dutifully plodding on the Path to Righteousness, in spite of the temptations along the way like tender juicy grass that grew in plenty beside the Path.

There was one who was not an usher: Margeline, a girl, who, for that reason, probably, had not been awarded a willow whip: instead, she weaved from side to side along the Path, making careful observations of choir deposits, not to be trodden on. The other eye, of course, was on constant lookout for ripe blackberries, and she carried a wicker basket for them.

There was another: an usher-in-training, one would suppose. Lawrence was not an usher: at the tender age of four, he was privileged to walk comfortably at random. From time to time it proved to be difficult to maintain even the ponderous pace of the choir: at such times one or the other of the accommodating ushers would snatch him up and fling him, squealing with great delight, into the back of the wagon onto folded blankets placed there for just such a purpose.

And then there was the *mater.* Sarah jounced along in the wagon seat, never even smiling at the varied antics of her family, stolidly resisting any and all attempts at amusement. Her attitude had not improved as they joked their way westward; due partly, perhaps, to the discomfort of riding on a hard board in an unsprung wagon. She rode with little amusement in her heart and less on her face, but the uncomfortable wagon seat was her own choice; Elam wisely chose not to open any more wounds.

The chasm *between them was already wide enough.*

**

No one had any idea when they would actually arrive within the bounds of the Platte Purchase. They followed the meanderings of the left bank of the Missouri River, knowing that the Platte was *on* the left bank, impossible to overlook. However: Elam, a great studier of maps, had thoroughly digested any maps of the river he could get his hands on. He knew that, when they approached the southernmost tip of the Platte, the river began a broad sweep around to the right. At that point could be found a small intersecting stream conveniently called the Platte River, for which the Purchase itself had been named. His ears perked up when the Missouri began turning to the north: at the same place, a small stream appeared on the right.

Not long after the slow turn to the north, a comparatively sharp bend to the west followed. His senses now on high alert, ahead was a low bluff and an immense field of green grass waving in the wind.

The fabled bottom land!

A single wagon stood atop the bluff just at the point where the river made that sharp turn to the west. The preacher, the choir, the ushers, and the entire congregation drew to a halt behind the wagon on the bluff. The preacher couldn't tear his eyes from the field of grass.

Under the grass, the finest soil in the whole wide world.

All gathered around their leader to look down on the grass, rolling in the wind like an incoming tide.

All gathered, that is, but one. Sarah sat stiff-faced, looking away. She didn't appear to see anything: not the river, not the bluff, not the grass. And, most certainly, not Elam.

Watching her, he again saw the chasm in her drawn face, her hunched shoulders. The look of defeat.

For the famed bottom land was the land of miasma.

He gave up, at that point. Conceded. He loved her very much: at this moment, more than ever. Perhaps God intervened: the folks clustered around the wagon told him the good bottom land was already gone, settled by those that had come to this place before. He was too late.

Like the preacher on the mountain, Elam pointed the way: not to heaven, but to the east, where a dusty track wandered upward from the river to the hills. Away from the bottom land.

Disheartened, he quietly set off along the dusty track. The obedient choir, the cattle followed with hardly a grunt. Then the ushers: Little Lawrence, Thomas, Warren. Margeline and her basket. Sarah, still in the wagon.

Elam plodded upward on the track some five or so miles: far enough away from the river, he hoped, from where the *miasma* would lie in the low places according to those that knew, or claimed they knew.

*Above and beyond the foul air, the
poisonous vapors, the fetid swamp land.
The miasma that caused it, the nebula,
blown by the morning breezes mingled
with the mist, the poisonous breath of
creatures of the marshes.*

In time, on encountering a sizable creek, he paused
to drink, for the day had become warm. Following his
lead, the choir surged forward and mimicked the
preacher at the stream. Then the ushers, cautiously
upstream from the choir.

Others of the congregation apparently had their
reasons not to be thirsty on this warm day. Sarah sat
fiercely on the wagon seat: hostile, rigid as a poker.
Elam's misery deepened.

 Continuing up the track, they encountered a small
spring burbling from the ground, its water icy cold to
the touch. Elam took a tin cup from the back of the
wagon, filled it at the spring, handed it to Sarah.

She relented, thank God, and took the proffered
cup. A good, deep, hearty swallow. Then she smiled.

*Just a little smile, it was. But it was like a gift from
heaven.*

Flushed with a new happiness, he bent to grasp a
handful of soil and squeezed it hard in his fist. The
senses of a farmer approved: the soil was good. Still
with the good soil in his hand, he looked about him at
the forested glade in which they stood. *Not unlike the
glade his father had once chosen back in Berkshire
Corners.*

The imagination could not conceive a finer country—lovely, rolling, fertile, wonderfully productive, beautifully arranged for settlement, part prairie and part timber—peace and contentment reigned—the hills and prairies and the level places were alike covered with a black and fertile soil—I cannot recall seeing an acre of poor ground in Platte county...John Bidwell

They built a snug house with beautiful logs of oak that looked to be straighter and rounder than any logs anywhere else. (And heavier, they might have thought, but didn't say.) In the main room, they installed an enormous fireplace of stone, for winter would soon set in, and on this first high hill east of the plains, the winter wind would be fierce. Elam was delighted at the way everyone in the family worked together: Thomas helped him fell the trees, then, as at Mr. Paddy's mill on the Gasconade, they used the team of horses to drag the heavy logs to the chosen spot by the cool spring. Warren, it turned out, quickly became an expert at axing in the notches near the log ends. Margeline worked as hard as the men, towing a horse-pulled sledge loaded with mud from the creek for the caulking between the logs. Even Sarah perked up a bit with all the activity, perhaps swept away by the good humor of all, the laughs when the sledge spilled over, and the hilarious antics of mud be-spotted Margeline and Lawrence when they smeared as much on themselves as on the logs.

Elam prayed it would last.

1836, October 22: Sam Houston is sworn in as the first president of the Republic of Texas.

**

1837, January: Doctor John Marsh purchases the Rancho Los Meganos (13,316 acres at the foot of Mt. Diablo) from Jose Noriega for $300 in cowhides.

The house on the Platte was finished, enough of it, anyway, before the heavy onslaught of winter. They had brought from Illinois enough to feed themselves through the winter, along with the herd of cattle to nourish them with milk and meat. Come the Spring, the sacks of seed would then be planted in the beautiful soil to sprout and grow, then the cycle would begin again. Elam felt a greater faith in the power of his prayers for a happy and prosperous family in this new place. When the autumn ripened, he roamed the hills nearby, collecting the brilliantly colored oak leaves to cheer Sarah as best she could be cheered.

1837, March 28: President Martin van Buren, exercising a codicil in the Treaty of Prairie du Chien, proclaims the Platte Purchase to be a part of the State of Missouri.

The terms of the Treaty with the Indians now stood fulfilled. The rights to a bit of land that had once belonged to the Indians had been transferred to the

State of Missouri, in unquestionable accordance with Supreme Court decision 21 U.S. 543, February 28, 1823, Johnson v. M'Intosh, which lay down the foundations of aboriginal title in the United States. (In actual fact, the Indians had been twice remunerated for the Platte Purchase: in 1830 and again in 1837. Although Johnson v. M'Intosh addresses Legal title to the land, it avoided the subject of coercion, such as an onrush of "squatters.")

> *1837, May 10: The "Panic of 1837" begins when New York City banks suspend specie (money in coin) payments, marking the beginning of a seven year recession. Banks collapse, businesses fail, unemployment rages as high as 25%. Inflation becomes rampant. "Oregon Fever" grows.*

> *1837: Peter Burnett's partnership fails. Now $15.000 in debt, he resumes his study of law and opens his own practice. He edits the Liberty, Missouri newspaper The Far West, for which he receives no salary. He joins a debating club to improve his speaking ability. His law practice prospers.*

> *1838, October 27: Missouri Governor Lilburn Boggs issues Missouri Executive Order 44, known as the "Extermination Order," which states "...the Mormons must be treated as*

> *enemies, and must be exterminated or*
> *driven from the State if necessary for*
> *the public peace...” (Rescinded by*
> *Governor Christopher Bond June 25,*
> *1976.)*

Isaac and Margaret Allen moved in two miles or so higher up the hill. Isham and Mary Ann Cox, a half-mile to the west. The neighborhood was beginning to fill up. Then, on a beautiful morning in June, 1839, an alert-looking, very young man, with a very short and very dashing beard, arrived on the doorstep. His name was, he said, John Bidwell. He also said he was a school teacher and therefore had no money, but he thought he might settle in this beautiful place if he could find a farm. He might also, he said, start a school. Of course, he had no money to do either. Then he said he supposed it didn't take much education to teach a country school at that period in Missouri, which might not have been a very astute thing to say.

> *"I taught school there (Weston) in all*
> *about a year. My arrival was in June,*
> *1839..."*

> *1839: Peter Burnett serves as defense*
> *counsel with Alexander W. Doniphan*
> *for Joseph Smith and other Mormon*
> *leaders in the Liberty jail. When the*
> *Grand Jury finds cause for indictment,*
> *the defense moves for a change in*
> *venue. While being moved, the*
> *prisoners escape to Illinois.*

> *Burnett is appointed District Attorney and relocates to Weston. However: his income is inadequate to repay his indebtedness and he obtains the permission of his creditors to move to Oregon.*

> *1839: John Sutter arrives to establish his New Helvetia [Sutter's Fort] settlement at the confluence of the Sacramento and American Rivers.*

Bidwell's qualifications, or lack of same, mattered little to Elam. He took an instant liking to the young man, perhaps because of his apparent honesty. The affinity was mutual; in spite of the difference in their ages, or perhaps because of it, the two of them launched simultaneously into the sort of conversation where one begins to speak even before the other has finished. They had, after all, similar backgrounds: born in New York, moved to Ohio, and ultimately, to this most remote western edge of the United States. It at once appeared that both had been bitten with the same wanderlust bug. Such a meeting happens rarely in a lifetime: they stood in the doorway engaged in furious conversation until either could hardly stand any longer.

Elam explained that his new friend might be able to obtain a farm as Elam himself had, simply by squatting on the land; it took no funds. As far as a school, why, a school was exactly what was needed in Weston. And such a vivacious fellow as John Bidwell might just be able to take up a collection, might he not?

Resourceful fellow that he was, impecunious or not, Bidwell somehow managed to build a schoolhouse directly across the road from where they stood. At that point, neither of them would suppose that this twenty-year-old presumed school teacher, wildly energetic or not, might one day decide to become President of the United States.

> *"...taught school there in all about a year. I got a claim, and proposed to make it my home..."*

(It would not have been technically possible for him to "get a claim" in 1840 because the Preemption Act of 1841 had not yet been approved. Furthermore, he would not have been twenty-one years old at the time, as would be required by the Act. Nevertheless he did manage to build a schoolhouse.) He then states:

> *"In the following summer, 1840...I concluded to take a trip to St. Louis...while I was gone a man "jumped" my claim,...he was a bully— had killed a man in Callaway County— and everybody seemed afraid of him...unfortunately for me, he had the legal advantage...I lost about everything I had..."*

He had no claim, so it couldn't have been jumped. The man accused of "jumping the claim" was Colonel Bethel Allen, who (later) filed for and received a legal grant for the southwest one-quarter of Section twenty-nine, Township fifty-four north, Range thirty-five west, Fifth Principal Meridian. And it had a schoolhouse on it.

Nevertheless, it does appear that Bidwell had traveled to St. Louis, and that, upon his return, he found that Colonel Allen, seeing no one there, had settled on the land with the schoolhouse. At which point, Bidwell begins to board at Elam's house and continues to teach at the schoolhouse. He relates:

> *"In November or December of 1840, while still teaching school in Platte County, I came across a Frenchman named Roubidoux, who said he had been to California...his description of California was of the superlative degree favorable, so much so that I resolved if possible to see that wonderful land..."*

Bidwell went on to explain that he and the Frenchman formed an organization they called the "Western Emigration Society." They soon had about five hundred names of people indicating interest, along with many letters of inquiry. Bidwell continued:

> *"Our ignorance of the route was complete. We knew that California lay west, and that was the extent of our knowledge...an intelligent man with whom I boarded—Elam Brown— possessed a map that showed...a long lake...with two outlets, both running into the Pacific Ocean...he advised me*

> *to take tools along to make canoes, so*
> *that if we found the country so rough*
> *that we could descend one of these*
> *rivers to the Pacific."*

(A mysterious lake with two rivers descending to the Pacific Ocean appears on "A map of Mexico, Louisiana, and the Missouri Territory, East and West Florida, Georgia, South Carolina & part of the Island of Cuba," by John H. Robinson, M.D. This huge map, which sold for $15 a copy, was more accurate for Florida and Cuba than it was for plotting a route to California. The Bonneville Expedition of 1832, of which Joseph Walker was a member, found the map to be so inaccurate that it was withdrawn from further publication.)

Back at the Brown Ranch, disaster had struck earlier:

> *1840, May 29: Surveyors partition the*
> *"Public Lands" into Townships,*
> *Ranges, and Sections.*

A decent enough looking fellow named Jesse Applegate knocked on Elam's door. He was, he said, a "United States Deputy Surveyor," and he had come to partition the "Public Lands." Elam was most familiar with Public Land Surveys, having lived in Sections on numerous occasions in Illinois. He welcomed the fellow and bid him to proceed.

Elam followed in the surveyors' footsteps, and was much alarmed when it was declared that the south line of Section 29 ran right through the middle of several of his cultivated fields. The spring, their source of cooking and drinking water, lay some hundred feet north of the line; the house, some two hundred feet. At least, he was safe in that regard!

It wasn't until July of that year that a real problem developed. The summer of 1840 began early, turned warmer than usual, and progressed without noticeable rainfall. By July, the sole branch that flowed through the property, which provided the drinking water for all the stock, had gone dusty-dry. A much larger branch, flowing with water, ran through the land to the west. Upon inspection, Elam determined that it was located on the land of Isham Cox. He continued on to Isham's house, and was and was immediately instructed to, by all means, allow his stock to drink of the ready supply of water.

> *1840, October 3: Isham Cox visits Elam, bringing with him a very official looking document.*

The document stated that it was an "Indenture" between E. Brown and Isham and Mary Ann Cox: "Isham Cox and Mary Ann Cox...in consideration of...five hundred dollars...grant...equal undivided half of the south west quarter of section twenty nine in Township fifty four North, Range thirty five West, containing eighty acres more or less, together with all and singular the appurtenances therewith belonging....unto the said Elam Brown..."

(THE INDENTURE HAD PROBLEMS

The Indenture, dated October 3, 1840, was technically invalid, for the United States still owned the property. (Many transactions occurred prior to the granting by the United States.)

The land was ultimately conveyed to John Martin and Isam (sic) Cox on May 1, 1846.

Description calls for "equal undivided half" which would indicate a half interest in the total ownership (160 acres) with "all and singular appurtenances."

The description then calls for "Eighty acres."

The Indenture was subsequently filed for record August 4, 1845.)

> *1841, May 19: The Bartleson-Bidwell Party, 61 travelers, departs Sapling Grove, Missouri, for California, guided by Tomas "Broken Hand" Fitzpatrick. Included in the Party was Joseph Chiles, making his first trip west.*

> *1841, June 18: Governor Juan Bautista Alvarado grants El Sobrante [Sacramento County, California], 11 leagues (47,827 acres) to John Sutter, which he names "New Helvetia."*

> *1841, September 4: The **Distributive Preemption Act** (27 Cong., Ch. 16; 5 Stat. 453) is approved. It was designed to "appropriate the proceeds of the sales of public lands...and to grant 'pre-emption rights' to individuals"*

> *who were already living on federal lands (commonly referred to as "squatters").*

The Pre-Emption Act changed everything. Section 10 stated: "...every person...over the age of twenty-one years, and being a citizen of the United States...who since the first day of June, A.D. eighteen hundred and forty, has made...a settlement...on the public lands to which the Indian title had been...extinguished. And who has or shall erect a dwelling thereon, shall be...authorized to enter with the register of the land office...any number of acres not exceeding one hundred and sixty, or a quarter section of land...upon paying to the United States the minimum price of such land..."

> *1841, November 4: Bartleson-Bidwell Party, the first wagon train to California, arrives at Dr. John Marsh's Rancho Los Medanos, having traveled down the easterly slope of the Sierra Nevada to Walker Lake and westerly to the San Joaquin Valley.) Bidwell presses on to Sutter's Rancho.*

Elam officially qualified as a squatter, however unappealing such a designation might be. According to Section 9 of the Pre-Emption Act, such a squatter might purchase a quarter section of land for a minimum price of one dollar and twenty-five cents per acre. *One hundred and sixty acres of some of the finest farmland in the world.* Elam Brown submitted his claim for the Southeast Quarter of Section 29, Township 54 North, Range 35 West, Fifth Principal Meridian. The price of the submittal was two hundred dollars. *Not free. But not bad, either.*

> *1842, January 1: John Bidwell begins the dismantling of Fort Ross, purchased in 1841 by John Sutter through his agent Peter Burnett from the Russian American Company for $19,800 in notes and gold.*

> *1842, May: Lansford W. Hastings, a twenty-three-year-old lawyer from Mount Vernon, Ohio, joins an Oregon emigration party captained by Dr. Elijah White and piloted by Thomas Fitzpatrick.*

> *1842, May 6: Former Missouri Governor Lilburn Boggs is shot in an assassination attempt. Orrin Porter Rockwell, a close associate of Joseph Smith, Jr. is apprehended, but acquitted of the charge.*

> *1842, June 10: Lieutenant John C. Fremont of the Corps of Topographical Engineers sets off from Chouteau's Landing, near present-day Kansas City, to survey an emigrant route to South Pass through the Rocky Mountains.*

1842, September: Commodore Thomas ap Catesby Jones occupies Monterey, California, thinking the United States and Mexico were at war.

1842, October 19: Commodore Thomas ap Catesby Jones discovers war has not developed and restores the town to the Mexican authorities with full apologies and ceremonies. He loses his command.

(It is recorded in the army journals that a series of powerful storms struck western Missouri in 1843, and that one of the worst of them arrived early in the morning of January 8. For hours, wind and snow aplenty lashed its mighty teeth against the first natural obstacle after a thousand miles of unobstructed plain; the ridge of hills that lay just east of the Missouri River.)

Elam lay snugly but not necessarily comfortably in his warm bed, for it was greatly possible that such a wind as this might do great damage not only to the stock in the fields, but to the house itself. Without a doubt: Margeline and Lawrence had done a first-rate job of chinking between the logs: nevertheless, with the snow flashing past the dark windows like white sheets torn from a main mast, great damage might be done. Indeed, the wind blew so hard as to creak the solid log house as if it were a ship at sea.

The storm had been raging for most of the night: then he heard roof shingles ripping away, to be hurled into oblivion somewhere. Happy with that success, the wind dropped a branch on the wounded roof, then struggled to tear the house completely apart, to return its logs to the forest that was there before these intruders from elsewhere had leveled those once-mighty trees and fashioned them into something hardly like trees.

Still, he lay half-awake in that delicious dream-like state rarely found; half in, half out of sleep. He let his thoughts return to Christmas, the Christmas of '42, now two weeks past. The happiest Christmas ever.

That Christmas had fallen on a Sunday. A cold Sunday, it was. Probably not as cold as today, but cold enough to lighten the blowing snow into a fine white powder that stuck to the front of the house like a fine white coat. He lay there, just thinking and dreaming. At last, it seemed that things were beginning to run in his favor, and it was about time: already, he was forty-two years old.

It seemed that Christmas was extra special that year: even a cedar bough became special. Thomas found the branch in the deep snow behind the house, apparently broken off by the storm. With an exaggerated demonstration of great care, he brought the fallen bough it inside and impetuously arranged it on the mantel as if it had there met its end. Margeline at once decorated the poor fallen branch with hair ribbons, after which Father Elam solemnly read aloud the Christmas Story from Luke. Then they all stood, held hands and reverently sang Dr. Watts' Cradle Hymn to the branch:

Hush, my dear, lie still and slumber,
Holy angels guard thy bed,
Heavenly blessings without number,
Gently falling on thy head.

Even Sarah snapped out of her funk after the little performance. She had recently stopped complaining about moving to The Platte and the dangers of the *miasma,* perhaps because Elam no longer dared to express his displeasure that they hadn't filed their Preemption claim for the fantastic bottom-land down by the river. The pact between them apparently worked, for Sarah reverted to her old self: after the community sing, she paraded from the kitchen with a platter of the delicious mince pies she was so expert at creating. She'd had a big smile, too. Just like old times. *She looked just like the pretty little thing he'd married back at Apple Creek in '23.*

He stirred in the warm bed. That big smile was two weeks ago.

Right after Christmas, she reverted back to her "new" self.

Her complexion began to change. Her face had swollen a little: not much, but a little. Probably, no one even noticed it except him. And he'd noticed it only because he'd started to watch her more closely.

The bed began to shake, just a little, as if a cat had jumped on the mattress and begun to wash himself. *Elam froze.* At once the semi-dreams, the recollections, halted. The bed quieted for a moment, then shook again, as if the wind had begun to rock the house. He knew that couldn't be the case, and reached out to touch her. *He felt the heat of her body before his hand even got close.*

A moment later, her thin body began to shake so badly the bed covers fell away: he drew them back, tucking them in around her shoulders.

He became badly frightened.

Sarah was ill.

Really terribly, terribly ill.

Frantic now, he bounded from the warm bed into the cold dark, searching for a candle and a lucifer to light it. His distress heightened when he saw her face: much more swollen now, cheeks flushed red, teeth chattering, eyes frightened.

He was devastated.

She had the ague.

The rest of the day passed in a blur. Later, he would recall awaking Thomas, giving him instructions to ride to Weston, bring the doctor.

He sent Warren into the dark night up the hill to the Allen house: Margaret had a lot of children: she would know how to deal with this.

While he waited for the mercy missions to return, he raced back and forth between the suffering Sarah and the cold fireplace, laboring to breath it back to life, for the house was freezing cold.

Warren returned first. He brought Margaret, who immediately rushed to Sarah and began whatever ministrations women always are able to apply.

She pushed the men out of the room: Elam and Isaac repaired the puny fire.

Next, Thomas burst through the door in a frigid wave of air, but without a doctor. The doctor, he said, was unavailable, but the doctor's wife had given him remedies that, she said, was all her husband could have done in any case.

There was *Calumel.* The label on the bottle said it would "break" the fever, but it just smelled like Cod Liver Oil. He spooned some through Sarah's resisting lips, unsure that any of it arrived where it was intended to arrive.

There was *Sappington's Anti-Fever Pills,* bitter smelling, and, surely, bitter tasting.

Margaret had brought a better balm: *Sassafras Tea* made from roots she had brought from her own kitchen. Of the medications, it was most obvious that the latter was by far the most satisfactory to the patient.

.

In time, Margaret returned to her own family, for nothing else could be done. Elam sat with Sarah, holding her fevered hand, mopping her fevered head while Margeline bravely took over the kitchen and fed the boys. Elam had no appetite.

The day turned to night. The snow fell. The wind blew.

He sat with her all night long, knowing it was all to no avail..

The shaking stopped early in the dark morning of January 9, 1843.

Sarah was gone.

Elam sobbed.

Elam cursed, the very first time in his life.

It was he who had brought her to this place of miasma.

SIX

THOMAS

1843-1846

1843, February 3: The United States Senate passes the "Distribution-Preemption Act," which would grant free land in Oregon Country: 640 acres to each immigrant and 160 acres to each child.
Construction begins on Sutter's Fort at New Helvetia. John Bidwell becomes General Manager for John Sutter for a salary of $25 per month.

On the first of May in the year of our Lord 1843, streams of wagons flowed into Independence, Missouri like an invading army. These were not the big, hulking Conestoga wagons that would arrive a few years later. These were ordinary farm wagons, pulled from the fields: only the canvas covers likened those that came after ward. There were a hundred wagons, some guessed. A hundred and twenty, guessed others.

Troops of people, like battalions of infantry, marched with the wagons rolling in: scores of families. Fathers, mothers, children, all afoot, save the very ill or the very young or the very old.

How many people? Seven hundred? A thousand? The guessers were at it again.

Then there were cattle: vast trumpeting herds of cattle, all at full bellow. How many? One observer got it right: *a helluva lot.*

They gathered and marched for the free land that was to be made available "Out West" in the Oregon Country. Back in 1836, Senator Thomas Hart Benton had declared: "Nobody will go three thousand miles to settle a new country unless he gets land by it." And it appeared he was right.

The Great Migration of '43 had begun.

Thomas Brown stood beside his wagon and watched the assemblage grow. The wagon wasn't *his,* actually: it belonged to Mr. Peter Hardeman Burnett, Esquire, Circuit Attorney, Platte County, Missouri, resigned as of March 30, 1843; Thomas was going to drive the wagon to Oregon Country in return for bed and board.

Like so many during the period, Mr. Burnett had found himself in financial difficulty. Also, like the others, he decided to head west in search of a fresh start. Trouble was, he had a sick wife and a bunch of children and therefore needed several wagons to haul all his stuff across the plains. And that's where Thomas came in.

Thomas had visited Mr. Burnett in his Weston office because he had heard the lawyer intended to migrate west to Oregon Country.

And that, Thomas had decided, was exactly what Father needed.

Father, devastated since Mother's death from the *ague* just a few months earlier, was a changed man, and doubly devastated because he heaped all the blame for her death on himself. The ague, everyone knew, was caused by the *miasma* found near bottom lands beside rivers.

Father, after all, had insisted that they emigrate to the Platte Purchase. Mother had resisted the move, and the reason she resisted it was because she so feared the deadly *ague* caused by the *miasma.*

It was ridiculous, of course. After all, the *ague* was everywhere: even in New York City. Even California, they said. Father ignored that. It was his fault that she got the *ague* from the *miasma* because he had forced her to move to the Platte.

And that was that.

In actual fact, they hadn't lived on the bottom land where the fogs and the *miasma* were most prevalent, because *that very best soil in the whole wide world* had already been settled on by the time they arrived. They had to settle in the hills, miles from the bottom land and the fog. But that didn't matter: she still got the *ague*.

So it was his fault and no one could tell him anything different.

Maybe it was just another bit of bad luck. He had never been one of those people that simply stumbled into good luck at every turn. His luck always seemed to be the other way around. They had moved to the Platte, for example, because they weren't making it in Illinois. The position as Justice of the Peace helped a bit, but the job didn't pay much, and it took him away from the farm, which wasn't a good thing.

The Justice of the Peace job wasn't as bad as the lead mines, though. Oh, how he hated that work. They called it "mining," but it wasn't really mining. The lead was near the surface of the ground, and in the summer time, he and all the other farmers that were having a bad time travelled north to dig "badger holes," as they were called: in a month or so, a farmer could dig enough lead to see his family through the winter.

But how he hated that, the digging in the hot summer sun. Fighting the gnats. The gnats were so bad that the diggers called them "lead bugs."

There seemed to be a perpetual survival problem: not because his father didn't work hard, or because he was a poor farmer, which he certainly was not. There seemed to be always problems with either the weather or the national economy. If the weather was too dry, the crops wouldn't grow. If the rains came, the crops were good but the economy was sour. Or the rains wouldn't quit and the crops flooded out.

Thomas was well aware of all the problems of a farmer, as children often are, however much their parents might think the whispering in the kitchen kept the secrets from them.

When they arrived too late on the Platte after the highly prized "bottom land" had already been taken, Father swallowed hard and headed for the hills. The still-available hill land had been good, but not as good as the flat land close beside the river. Then there was the problem of adequate water for the stock; the "branch" (as they call a creek in Missouri) dried up when summer arrived. So he purchased rights to Isham's "branch" next door, although the purchase could be least afforded. (If there ever *was* a time when *anything* might be better afforded.) Finally, the government surveyors cut away two of the better fields because they lay on the other side of the Section line they staked.

No, it couldn't be said that Father had a lot of good luck. And now bad luck was knocking at the door again. Thomas wanted to help him get away from the farm on the Platte, where the bad luck seemed to come without end. All the talk was about moving to a place they called "Oregon Country." It was a place Father seemed to be much interested in: he and Mr. Bidwell had often talked into the night about this fabled place. Father seemed to be lost after Mr. Bidwell headed out.

There was a big problem: Father didn't actually own the Platte farm yet. Although he had settled on the Platte Purchase six years ago and the surveyors marked out the Sections three years ago, title to the land hadn't actually arrived.

And no one had any idea about when the magic day might arrive. And if the wait dragged on too long, all the good land in Oregon Country might be taken, and a move west would solve nothing. They were stuck.

After giving the problem considerable thought, Thomas one day arrived at a solution. Or thought he had. *He could go to Oregon Country himself, find some good land, then lay claim himself, for the family!*

Problem was: he had no idea how he would do these things. Then, on February 27, 1843, Mr. Burnett spoke about the Oregon question at the courthouse. He had said that he, himself, advocated "going thither."

Thomas recalled that Mr. Burnett had spoken on the Oregon question at the court house on February 27, 1843, and had advocated "going thither." Mr. Burnett was a lawyer. *And lawyers know everything!* Thomas raced down the hill to Weston and the lawyer's office.

Peter Hardeman Burnett (who, somewhere along the way, had added a second "t" to his name because he believed it looked more distinguished with two) had, until very recently, been the "Circuit Attorney" in Platte County.

Mr. Burnett didn't look particularly distinguished, even with the double "t" in his name. He was a tall and rather grumpy-looking man, but had a strong voice and a glib tongue. His office was at the moment somewhat barren, for which he was apologetic, stating that he had just resigned his position and was soon moving to Oregon Country. This bit of news hugely excited Thomas.

It turned out that this tall grumpy-looking man was most gracious and talkative (perhaps because his wily mind had just recognized Thomas as a solution to one of his own problems) and informed his visitor in a pleasant southern voice that he had studied law on his own, had worked as a store-keeper, that he had eventually bought the store and subsequently lost it along with a great deal of money before going into the practice of law.

Thomas was amazed that such a total stranger would care to divulge such a quantity of rather uncomfortable information about himself, and was astounded to learn that the man had become a lawyer by the simple process of studying some law books on his own!

Somewhat uncomfortably, Thomas relayed his desire to go to Oregon Country himself and lay claim to land that he could then convey to Father. The lawyer at once tossed onto his desk a copy of the *Bonneville Herald,* dated March, 1843, which explained in brief newspaperish lingo that a "Distribution-Preemption Act" had recently been passed by the U.S House of Representatives which would entitle emigrants to Oregon Country 640 acres to each person, plus 160 acres to each child. Since Mr. and Mrs. Burnett had six children, the family could receive 2240 *free* acres, giving him enough value to pay off his debts and start over. Thomas' nimble mind quickly calculated that, if his own plan worked, the Brown family, with four children, could accumulate 1280 acres! *Free!*

Thomas struggled to contain his enthusiasm and skipped over the statement in the paper that Oregon Country was not yet a part of the United States and that the Act therefore had no validity, even if the U.S. Senate passed it and the President signed it. It was inevitable, in any case, he might have concluded. *And he must move quickly, or lose the opportunity.*

The lawyer fell silent, as if exercising a legalistic rhetorical pause to permit Thomas' obvious excitement to thoroughly soak in before he proposed a *caveat emptor.*

Slowly shaking his head, a lawyerly way of explaining the *obvious* problem, that of little time. He said that, with such good terms offered for the free land, the world would rush in and grab up all the good stuff, leaving the junk for the fools that hesitated.

It was exactly the reason Father had missed out on *the best soil in the whole wide world.*

Then Mr. Burnett presented Thomas with an offer he couldn't refuse. The low lawyerly voice, accentuated in a pleasant southern drawl, suggested that Thomas might *do a man's service on the journey for bed and board.* That, he explained further was not at all an uncommon occurrence. *He merely wanted Thomas to drive one of the Burnett wagons to Oregon!*

Thomas rushed home to explain this extraordinary turn of events to Father; who, in his characteristic manner of speech, maintained that he could *never* rush into a decision on a matter of such importance.

But he approved the proposal on the very next morning.

And so, on May 8, 1843, a hundred or so wagons began to creak their way westerly from Independence to Fitzhugh's Mill amid general shouting, clapping of hands, loud *geeing* and *hawing* to direct the oxen. At Fitzhugh's Mill, the emigrants halted to hold the first organizational meeting of the "Oregon Emigrating Company."

Thomas was surprised to find the surveyor Jesse Applegate in the crowd, large as life. The giant of a man recognized him at once, recalling the survey years before on Father's land. An impressive, powerful man, Jesse was. Muscular and over six feet tall, he was a true surveyor: it was said he could easily walk sixty miles in a day, then do it again on the following day.

Traveling with Jesse were his wife Cynthia, her brother William Parker, his niece Harriet Williams, her husband Benjamin, Jesse's older brother Charles, and younger brother Lindsay. (Lindsay's claim to fame occurred in 1919, when the family lived in Spring Creek, Illinois. Then fifteen years old, he had played with a gangly boy named "Abe," later elected the sixteenth President of the United States.) The Applegate group took, altogether, four wagons, as well as a herd of livestock that included about eight hundred cattle.

The Company hired a guide known as "Captain Gantt," a former soldier and fur trader, to guide them as far as Fort Hall for a fee of one dollar per head. (By sheer chance, the crowd also included a missionary doctor named Marcus Whitman, who happened to be passing through Independence. Dr. Whitman, then stationed near the Hudson's Bay post of Ft. Walla Walla on the Columbia River, agreed to guide them the remainder of the way.)

> *1843, May 20: Chiles-Walker Party, the second wagon train to California. Joseph Chiles departs Westport, Missouri with a company of thirty men, six women, three wagons, and machinery to build a mill. They meet a larger Party headed for Oregon, some of which joined them, and later encounter Joseph Walker, who agrees to guide them. They split at Ft. Boise: Chiles and thirty horsemen continue by way of Pitt River to Sutter's Fort, arriving November 2. Walker takes the southerly route through Walker Pass, arriving at Gilroy's Rancho on December 3, the second wagon train to arrive in California.*

1843, May 29: The second Fremont expedition, under Lieutenant John C. Fremont, leaves Kansas City for an accurate survey of the emigrant route to Oregon Country.

After the Company crossed the Kansas River, it halted for a subsequent meeting, at which Peter Burnett was elected captain of the huge train of wagons. That captaincy was short-lived, however: he soon resigned the position because of a growing dissension about the very large herd of livestock, which, he maintained, would slow the train and make night guard duty difficult.

The train was judiciously divided into two units: one, the "light column" (without the livestock) to be captained by a William Martin. It was no surprise that Jesse Applegate was chosen to captain the slow "cow column," for he owned two hundred head of cattle himself. (It was later noted that the division of the train made little difference after all: the two columns traveled much as one anyway, typically camping each night within shouting distance of each other.)

1843, June 20: The lawyer Lansford W. Hastings emigrates to California from Oregon.

On August 27, 1843, the train arrived at Fort Hall, a Hudson's Bay trading post in present-day Idaho. There they rested for several days and made repairs to the equipment. Captain Richard Grant, the officer in charge of the post, advised them to leave the wagons behind and to continue on horseback, because the trail ahead was deemed to be impassable for wagons. Part of the company did exactly that: they left their wagons at the fort and continued their trek with pack animals. Sixteen families gave up on Oregon Country entirely and diverted to California. The remaining wagons, including those of the Burnetts and the Applegates, dismissed Captain Grant's suggestion and forged ahead with their wagons.

Decision time came when they arrived at Fort Walla Walla on October 16, 1843. Some struggled on beside the Columbia River until the trail narrowed at The Dalles, where they halted to construct makeshift boats. Jesse, along with his brothers and their families who likewise were in the Company, made the fateful decision to leave the stock and the wagons with Hudson's Bay Company at the fort and to proceed by boat from there.

Lieutenant Fremont and his Topographical Corps happened to be at Fort Walla Walla when this last vestige of the wagon train arrived. He noted that he observed "...Mr. Applegate as a man of considerable resolution and energy..." as his troop constructed Mackinaw Boats of driftwood logs pulled from the river. Upon completion of the construction, the boats were loaded and launched from the Walla Walla canoe landing.

The government surveyors watched a horrific event from the river's east bank on November 6, 1843. Helpless to assist, they saw one of the boats capsize in the rapids, spilling the occupants into the raging river.

Lost were Jesse's oldest son, and Warren, the son of Jesse's brother. Both boys were nine years old.

The tragic event had a lasting effect on Jesse and his brother Lindsay: they vowed to find a better way into Oregon Country so others would not suffer such a tragedy.

The remaining members of the Company struggled into Oregon City on December 1, 1843. Actually, they but passed through that western terminus of the fabled Oregon Trail, hardly even pausing, on their way up the Willamette River to the old Methodist mission ten miles above Salem.

They were at the end of their rope, as well as the end of their trail. Peter Burnett wrote, "...by the time we reached the distant shores of the Pacific, after a slow wearisome journey of about two thousand miles, our little means were exhausted, and we had to begin life anew, in a new country...for the first two years after our arrival, our great difficulty was to procure provisions..."

Fortunately, Dr. John McLoughlin, governor of Hudson's Bay Fort Vancouver, needed a surveyor. Surveyors were in short supply during Oregon Country's early history, so Dr. McLoughlin was more than delighted when he discovered that one of the new emigrants was a much experienced member of that ancient profession. He welcomed Jesse Applegate with open arms.

Dr. McLoughlin, like many of the English and Canadian residents of the area, had been much disturbed by the recent passage of the bill in the United States Senate to grant pre-emption rights to early settlers. The bill would have no authority as long as Oregon Country was under joint control of the United States and the United Kingdom, but the overtones were ominous. In order to protect his rights in the frightful possibility of American control, Dr. McLoughlin decided that he should file some land claims "just in case," which had been prepared by Lansford Hastings back in 1842.

Hastings had arrived at Fort Vancouver in September of that year. This gentleman, impeccably dressed in the most fashionable suit of clothes in spite of his recent two thousand mile journey in a wagon from Missouri, and sometimes described as "a bright, handsome, strong-jawed opportunist" was exactly what the doctor ordered.

And the doctor was exactly what the lawyer ordered. Together, they planned not simply a plot of land for a farm, but an entire *City!* Oregon City was on its way almost before Lansford Hastings clambered down from his wagon.

But the new city was only on paper, for the lawyer was only a lawyer. A *surveyor* was needed to bring the city to reality *on the ground.* Then, in June of 1843, the estimable Mr. Hastings set off for California to write a book about how terrible Oregon was!

Fortunately, Jesse Applegate had brought with him from Missouri his surveyor's magnetic compass: the old-faithful, reliable *Rittenhouse.* And a good, serviceable surveyor's chain. To perform the work of staking out the claim, he only needed an assistant: a surveyor cannot work alone. Fortunately, his friend Thomas was available.

Thomas, well-pleased by this circumstance, at once posted a letter to his father back in Weston to announce that he had arrived safely in Oregon Country and had already found employment.

1844, February: John Bidwell purchases Rancho Ulpinos [near Rio Vista.]

1844, March 8: US Army Captain John C. Fremont arrives in California with topographical survey crew to map overland routes.

1844, May: Peter Burnett purchases a claim on the Tualatin Plain. He finds farming a difficult proposition and manages to become elected as a member of the Legislative Committee of Oregon. He introduces a measure to prohibit slavery in Oregon. If any slaves are not removed within 3 years, they are to receive 20-39 lashes, which action is strongly criticized. (Article 4 of Organic Laws of Oregon. The whipping portion was repealed in December.)

1844, May 22: The Stephens-Townsend-Murphy Party, 50 travelers in a train of 40 wagons, departs Iowa. Headed for California, they are guided by mountain

*men   Caleb   Greenwood   and   Isaac
Hitchcock.*

*1844: Governor Manuel Micheltorena
grants [Johnson's Rancho], 22,197
acres, Yuba County, California to Pablo
Gutierrez, sold to William Johnson in
1846.*

*1844: Governor Manuel Micheltorena
grants Rancho Catacula (Two leagues:
8,546 acres), Napa County, California,
to Joseph Chiles.*

Jesse and Thomas staked out that first portion of
Oregon City to be claimed, as described by John
McLoughlin: "... *so much of the town as lies between
Washington Street and the River, surveyed in the
Spring of 1844 by Jesse Applegate...*"

Thomas, having a certain quickness of mind and a
bent toward mathematics, was an apt pupil: he readily
comprehended Jesse's explanation of the workings of
the surveyor's compass and the surveyor's chain. The
magnetic compass, he would have learned, indicated
the direction of a course, measured in degrees and
minutes of a degree from north or south as modified to
east or west. The (Gunter's) chain was not really a
chain at all: but a hundred links of wire totaling sixty
feet in length. That basic information would start a
whole new career.

Messrs. Frank Pettygrove and General A.L.
Lovejoy, then engaged in "merchandising" in Oregon

City, in 1843 had received an offer from a John P. Overton to sell his claim of 640 acres "12 miles down the river" for $50 in "store plunder," as there was little money in coin at the time. On inspection, it was determined that the offer to sell should be accepted. Pettygrove and Lovejoy required surveying and engineering work relative to a road to the new town they felt would be necessary. They contacted Jesse Applegate in early 1844.

Jesse, still much disturbed because of the tragic accident to his family on the river, felt he had other important work that needed to be done: the search for a southern approach to Oregon Country without the dangerous route down the Columbia River. He loaned his surveyor's compass and chain to Thomas, suggesting that he proceed with the work since he had had the experience in "surveying Oregon City," as he put it.

Thomas therefore was pleased to "survey Portland." Although it could be assumed from that statement he had surveyed the entire city, the first requirement was merely to stake eight blocks of lots along First and Second Streets between Jefferson and Washington Streets. That portion, completed in October, 1844, netted him $100 each from Pettygrove and Lovejoy.

Thomas Brown, now perhaps the sole active surveyor in all of Oregon Country, continued to practice his new profession throughout the area, often living in a tent on the various work sites, which gained him the title "itinerant surveyor." He dashed off a new letter to his father to tell him of the new role, and, although he was now considered to be "itinerant," he could always be reached at Portland.

He kept a surveyor's eagle eye out for farmland, regularly posting new accounts of decent locations to Father, although he was never certain that any of his letters arrived.

He also began to consider studying for the law, as well. The law, after all, was closely associated with surveying. *Peter Burnett had studied for the law all by himself, he had said. Why not Thomas?* Furthermore, the law could still be practiced in heavy rain, which made surveying difficult. It rained a lot in Oregon.

But the law could be practiced in the rain.

It could be studied in the rain, too.

If one had a tent.

1844, November 14: The Stephens-Townsend-Murphy Party reach Truckey's [Donner] Lake. Faced with the precipitous wall of granite ahead of them, a portion of the Party turn south on horseback to seek a more amenable route and eventually make their way to Sutter's Fort. The remainder manage, with great difficulty, to surmount the Pass with five of the wagons after ten days' hard labor, by unloading the wagons and hand-carrying the contents to the summit. They then fastened chains to the tongues of the empty wagons, which the double-teamed cattle pulled while the men lifted over a series of granite steps. The Party becomes the third wagon train to arrive in California.

SEVEN

WESTON

1845-1846

1845: U.S. Congress publishes a map of California and Oregon by Brevet Captain John C. Fremont, Topographical Corps.

Western Fever ramped up after Lansford Hastings published his *Emigrant's Guide to Oregon and California.* The *Guide* elaborately detailed all aspects of the proposed excursion, including details of the conveyance to be employed: "Whether wagons are new or old, it is, perhaps, preferable, always, to have the tires re-set, previous to leaving Independence..." the estimated time-span: "Those who go to Oregon, if they design to perform the journey in the ordinary time, of 120 days..." ancillary equipment: "...good wagon covers and tents, tent poles, axes, spades, and hoes, as well as strong ropes..." Special emphasis was placed on the departure time: "Emigrants should, invariably, arrive at Independence, Mo., on, or before, the fifteenth day of April, so as to be in readiness, to enter upon their journey, on, or before, the first day of May..." (Mr. Hastings apparently saw no need to mention that the traveler should also supply himself with an ample quantity of commas to be used for trade with Indians in short supply, should any such be encountered.)

Elam, like so many other adventurers at the time already keen to get going, would have eagerly devoured the *Guide.* However, faced with the knowledge that he would require not only the equipment and supplies listed in the book which he would need to purchase, but also an amount of money he would reckon to be $1,000 or thereabouts, no small amount. Times had been hard since Sarah's death (two years ago, already), and, while he had been able to survive satisfactorily, he had been unable to build up the required purse. There had been a strong flow of new emigrants into the Platte of late, but most were looking for land that was either free or nearly so.

One morning early in January, 1845, Joseph Jones knocked at the door and said he was looking for land but had no money. His timing was perfect. On January 13, 1845 Elam sold him seventy-four acres: the W 1/2 SW 1/4 S 29, T 54, R 35, and 4 perches off the W side E 1/2 SW 1/4 for the grand sum of ten dollars (Book C Page 168, Platte County Records). Elam would also have taken from Mr. Jones a promissory note in the amount of $1,000, probably in order to provide that worthy with free and clear title to land that could be used as equity to borrow funds for purchase of necessary farm equipment and stock.

The sale doubtlessly raised Elam's faith a bit. His faith, like the Western Fever, must have soared on March 1, 1845 when he sold two-hundred-and seventy-four acres to Barbara Ann and James Reese: certain tracts of land in SE 1/4 S 29, T 54, R 35 and E1/2 NE 1/4 and N 1/2 W 1/2 NE 1/4 S 32 T 54 R35 and E 1/2 SW 1/4 S29, T 54 R35 (Book C Page 392, Platte County Records) for three thousand eight hundred and ten dollars. It wasn't a bad deal for an initial investment of a $200.00 filing fee.

His prayers had been answered. Once again, he envisioned the church he would build. Now flushed with ready cash, he took Hasting's *Guide* from the shelf and listed the items he would need to purchase. On the very next day, Fremont's map in hand, he began canvassing the neighborhood for fellow adventurers, beginning with his good friend Isaac Allen.

> *1845, March 4: James K. Polk inaugurated president. His inflammatory campaign dialogue (54-40 or Fight) over the northern boundary of Oregon Country had brought the Royal Navy to full alert.*

Elam dashed off a letter to Thomas to tell him that the farm had been sold and that all the Browns remaining in Missouri would be making preparations to follow him to Oregon Country, which letter would be left at the Weston Post Office to await the next Company headed in that direction. (He fully realized that, since the next Company might very well be his own, it was possible that he would be delivering his own letter.)

> *1845, May 15: Peter Burnett is elected Judge of the Oregon Supreme Court.*

There was also the possibility of a third war between England and the United States over the status of the Oregon Country, which was still occupied jointly by the two countries. In addition, the potential annexation of the Republic of Texas by the United States might very well invite a war with Mexico. Elam allowed that he'd not worry about the political picture, but promised a very nice church.

> *1845, July 4: The Congress of the Republic of Texas endorses annexation to the United States.*

In spite of a considerable amount of reluctance by the wives, the husbands were so enthusiastic about going to Oregon that Elam returned to the Post Office to send a second letter to Thomas to inform him that they would likely depart Weston early in the month of May, 1846, in full accordance with Lansford Hastings directions. When he arrived at the Post Office, the Postmaster handed him a very impressive envelope that was near to bursting with officialness.

The envelope shouted **"WASHINGTON, D.C."** from its return-address area, loudly proclaiming that to even *touch* this all-important, hallowed document might be the cause for a **Penalty of Law.** Or worse.

It screamed **"OFFICIAL BUSINESS,"** should any vestige of doubt remain in the mind of the beholder. Elam guessed what the business might be about, but held the envelope for a long moment before cautiously tearing open the flap. In spite of all that caution, the contents, being a document as impressive as its envelope, floated imperiously to the floor. He looked down on the paper for a second long moment, but it didn't stir.

He knew that it was the government's response to his claim to land, filed so many years before.

The wait had been so long that he had already sold the land he had filed the claim for. What would happen now? What if the claim was now denied? It was unthinkable.

Why had the process taken so long? Well, of course, there would be a reasonable explanation. *There always was.* The government would have had to await a survey, in order to provide the location of the claim in order to describe it, wouldn't they?

Well. They had sent out a government surveyor Jesse Applegate, his name was. Way back in 1840.

Five years before.

Of course, they would then have to make an **"OFFICIAL"** review of the survey, wouldn't they? Before he could even *file* for the claim. The review took another two years.

Finally, in 1842, they sent word that all was well. At last, he filed the claim.

That was three years before.

In 1843, he thought the world was ending when Sarah died. He forgot all about claims and governments and such for a long, long time. Until he decided he had to move, to get away from the land that had caused all the trouble in the first place.

The **"OFFICIAL UNITED STATES GOVERNMENT"** made no mention of her death, and was probably unaware of it. As if it mattered, anyway, in the grand scheme of things. But two years had gone since 1843, and two years can be a long, long time. Elam was near his wits' end.

He so desperately wanted to leave the Platte, as far away as possible from this awful place that he had taken Sarah to die. But he couldn't simply go: first, he needed to sell the land to get the money to start over again, someplace else. Someplace far from here, *someplace that didn't have* miasma, someplace that didn't cause *death by ague.*

That was when he decided to go farther west, to Oregon Country. Thomas left *"to scout out a good location for them,"* he had said. And he was right. *Look what had happened right here in the Platte. Because they hadn't moved soon enough from Illinois, the river bottom land, the best soil in the whole wide world, had already been taken before they arrived.* So they filed a claim for land in the hills. Oh, the soil was pretty good in the hills, too. *But not the best in the whole wide world.*

When your hand is dealt, you gotta be quick or you'll lose. Certainly, he was good at losing, so he told Thomas, then a grown man at twenty, to go ahead to Oregon. *Elam had done the same thing himself after his father died.* He'd never forget that long walk to St. Louis.

Warren, now nineteen, would be next. Then Margeline. Already sixteen, she'd probably get married before long. Little Lawrence, only twelve, would probably stick around to help his father for a while, thank goodness.

The family was being chiseled away, bit by bit. The current patriarch, the one that wanted most to be gone, was out of luck.

He had rotten luck all his life, starting with that miserable logging job on the Gasconade. Then the share-cropping: where he did *all* the work for half the income. The moving about in Illinois, always looking on the lookout for something better. The need to scratch in the dirt for lead to make enough money to buy hay for the horses so they could plough the dry dirt and hope that the rains would come. And the rains didn't.

Then the farm on the Platte. The farm he forced on Sarah that *didn't* have the best dirt in the whole wide world.

But it did have the miasma.

And the miasma *took her away.*

> *1845, October 30: First Lieutenant Archibald H. Gillspie of the United States Marines meets with President James K. Polk. Entry in the President's diary reads: "I held a confidential conversation with Lt. Gillespie of the Marine Corps, about 8:o'clock p.m. on the subject of a secret mission on which he was about to go to California. His* secret *(emphasis added) instructions and the letter to Mr. Larkin, U.S. Consul at Monterey, in the Department of State, will explain the object of his mission."*
>
> *Gillespie sailed from New York City to Vera Cruz in the brig* Petersburgh, *spending part of the 24 days of stormy passage memorizing the dispatches to*

Larkin, which he then destroyed (emphasis added,)

And now, at last, the letter. He stooped to retrieve the official document from the floor, still exclaiming in its harsh governmental voice:

THE UNITED STATES OF AMERICA!

Then, even more pretentiously:

To all to whom these Presents shall come, Greeting: WHEREAS...

And his name, in softer tones, of course:

Elam Brown

Continuing:

# of Platte County, Missouri has

purchased land

Back to government speak:

according to the provisions of the Act of Congress of the 24th of April, 1820

Paraphrasing softly, his name once more:

Elam Brown.

Back to government:

BY THE PRESIDENT:

Then, at the bottom, softly:

James K. Polk

Certificate No. 544, Preemption No. 474: the **OFFICIAL TITLE** to one hundred and sixty acres in

Platte County, Missouri, *and signed by THE PRESIDENT!*

He pointedly ignored the additional hen scratching below the **PRESIDENT'S SIGNATURE** that could be construed to be the names of other inconsequential governmental aides like the Secretary of the General Land Office that might have actually signed the President's name.

At this exalted moment, Elam forgave the government for everything. The hallowed document was the actual Title to the land that he had waited so long for. Perhaps the extraordinarily long run of bad luck had taken a turn for the better. He would *definitely* start a church in the new place.

But the beautiful document changed nothing. He had already sold the property, after all. *Had* he? How could a person sell something he didn't own? Wouldn't that be fraudulent?

Now, a fresh worry.

Still. So many in the Platte had never actually owned that which they had sold! Although the Title could be considered after the fact, and therefore worthless for all practical purposes, it had some value, *because it bore the President's signature. Maybe.*

He wondered if Isaac Allen had received *his* Title yet. His closest friend, Isaac had decided to go to Oregon, as well, although Margaret didn't want to. It was a familiar story.

> *1845, December 8: United States offers Mexico $5 million for the western half of New Mexico, $10 million for a*

boundary giving San Francisco to the US, and $25 million for California.

1846, January 12: Mexico rejects the US offer. President Polk directs Brevet Brigadier General Zachery Taylor to move his army to the Rio Grande.

1846, January 20: US Marine Lieutenant Gillespie arrives in Guadalajara, purchases a sombrero, sash, and serape for $36.00 and saddle and bridle for $53.75.

1846, January 24: Fremont and his men visit with Mexican General Jose Castro at Monterey.

Elam's decision to visit his sisters in Ohio had been a sudden one, brought about one day when he had ridden down the hill to Weston to purchase some of the supplies that Lansford Hastings said were necessary. A big sternwheeler was tied to the main pier at the foot of First Street, busy with loading and off-loading. It was the biggest boat Elam had ever seen: he rode closer to the monstrous red paddlewheel for a closer look.

At the time, Weston was the westernmost town in the United States; hence its name. (Weston, *West-town.)* It was therefore the westernmost terminus of the new riverboat routes on the Missouri River, and the docks had become a busy place. Elam sat his horse for a few moments to admire the boat and to watch the travelers heading up the gangplank with their luggage.

It was thrilling to him that Weston, so remote from the rest of the world, was now so connected by the river to the great port of St. Louis. And New Orleans. And, by a stretch, London and Paris.

Even Ohio.

The boat was so magnificent he had difficulty tearing his eyes away. He realized that this would be a fine way to go to Ohio, to say goodbye. He'd probably never see his sisters again..

It sounded exciting. Down the Missouri to St. Louis; then another boat down the Mississippi to Cairo: and another up the Ohio to Columbus. What a marvelous modern transportation system, connecting all parts of the country! And it wasn't expensive, he had heard: a cabin, with all meals, cost only a ½ cent per mile.

With four months until May, he'd still have plenty of time to get ready for the trip to Oregon. Anyway, it was a little crowded at the Allen house. Margaret and Isaac were sharing not only their house, but also their pastures. The Allen cows hadn't yet complained about crowded pastures, but things were a bit tight in the house.

It might, Elam decided, be a good time to take a trip back to Ohio.

> *1846, March 8: Fremont and his men fortify the ridge atop Gavilan Peak. Three days later, they abandon the area and head for Oregon.*

1846, April 1: Imus-Aram Party, fifty travelers in twelve wagons, departs Apple River, Illinois, bound for California.

The soft hills were so green and beautiful that he wondered why he had ever left Ohio. How much simpler, how much easier, he reflected, life would have been if he hadn't headed west after his father died. The big house was still there, the grand house originally built by Byxbe's bricklayer, still used by the family, still a hotel, still a tavern.

His sisters still operated the hotel in the old house, and business was apparently flourishing. Only one big change had occurred since he'd left, when Sophsonia married Samuel Peck. He was a decent fellow, a local tanner, who was also handy with maintenance around the hotel.

The sisters, all four of them, vigorously launched into a heated campaign to convince Elam that he should forget his decision to march off into the great void of the West, where known and unknown diseases surely lurked, and that, in any case, savage hordes whacked off the heads of any that were able to resist all the natural calamities.

The sisters' eyes moistened up when they spoke of the nephews and the niece they had never even seen. But his most difficult time came when they asked after Sarah, for he became most overwrought and unable to compose himself.

They expeditiously returned the subject of conversation back to Oregon and seriously implored him to give up on the idea, to remain in Missouri if he so resolutely refused to return to Ohio. But that die had already been cast. The farm was sold: he had no remaining ties in Missouri. And Thomas, as the advance party, was already in Oregon awaiting the rest of his family. There could be no turning back.

At the Berkshire Cemetery, Elam was amazed at how the graveyard had grown. There he knelt before the white tombstones marking the resting place of father, mother, and brother and paused for a long, long time.

There was no stone for Sarah.

He had one foot in Ohio and one in Missouri and little attachment to either.

It was time to be movin' on.

>*1846, April 14: The Donner family and Reed family, 33 people in nine wagons, set off from Springfield, Illinois.*

Elam Brown

EIGHT

FORT JOHN [LARAMIE]

APRIL-JUNE 1846

1846, April 15: Donner-Reed families, thirty-three people in nine wagons, depart Springfield, Illinois. Aram/Imus Company, twelve families in twelve wagons, departs Jo Daviess County, Illinois for the Mexican Province of California.

1846, April 17: Lieutenant Gillespie arrives in Monterey aboard the 18-gun sloop of war Cyane, Captain William Mervine, after sailing to the Sandwich Islands ostensibly as a merchant bound for China. He relays the memorized instructions from the State Department to Consul Larkin, the gist of which [presumably] was to instruct Larkin to intrigue peacefully to get California to secede from Mexico and annex to the United States. Gillespie then rides to Yerba Buena [San Francisco] and meets with Vice-Consul William A. Leidesdorff, an old friend.

The first thing Elam did upon his return to Weston was to purchase a new wagon. Not a *new* wagon, but new to him. It had cost $50.00, which was a lot of money, but not as much as $75.00, the asking price of a new one. This wagon, he felt, would haul him the 2,000 miles to Oregon, but he was certain his old one would not. It had brackets for the bows already attached, over which cotton-hemp canvas treated with lots of linseed oil kept out the rain from overhead. Water barrels were already strapped onto platforms at the sides of the wagon. *It was a very fine wagon, indeed.*

When he showed up with his fancy "new" wagon, they at once elected him captain of the wagon train, which position, in spite of the "new" wagon, he reluctantly agreed to only if his good friend Isaac Allen served as co-captain. After some reluctance, Isaac agreed, but only if he could take along his tall case clock, to which request Elam readily agreed. The wagon train, therefore, should have been called the Brown-Allen Party, but modest Isaac demurred. Nevertheless, they remained warm friends, and together ferried The Brown Party, fourteen families in sixteen wagons, across the Missouri River at St. Joseph on the first day of May.

The timing of the river crossing was in exact accord with the *Emigrants' Guide to Oregon and California* by Lansford Hastings, which declared "Emigrants should...be in readiness to enter upon their journey on or before the first day of May..." thereby assuring "good pasturage...over those desolate and thirsty plains and being enabled to cross the mountains before the falling of mountains of snow..."

Hastings, a young lawyer from Mount Vernon, Ohio, traveled to Oregon Country in 1842, and to Mexican California in 1843, returning to the United States by ship in 1844. He published his *Emigrants' Guide* in 1845. Described as intelligent, active, and ambitious, but "of a selfish and arbitrary disposition," he was also said to have "visions of greatness and a penchant for grand schemes." The book stated that "...California was, beyond any doubt, one of the most delightful countries in the known world." Oregon, on the other hand, was a dark and dismal place filled with hostile Indians.

Undaunted, the Brown train nevertheless headed for Oregon Country.

> *1846, April 25: Lieutenant Gillespie travels by small boat to Sutter's Fort, where his thin disguise as a commercial traveler was exploded when a Mr. Loker told John Sutter that he had seen Gillespie many times at the Washington Navy Yard. Gillespie moves on to Lassen's ranch in search of Fremont.*

> *1846, May 9: Fremont meets Gillespie at his camp on the Klamath River in Oregon. They talk long and late around the campfire: it is presumed that Gillespie recited his memorized instructions from President Polk.*

1846, May 10: Donner-Reed Party crosses the Missouri River at Independence, Missouri. Boggs family departs from Indian Creek.

The Brown Party's first major disaster struck upon reaching the confluence of the North Platte River with the South Platte River, some three hundred miles west of St. Joseph.

It was yet the early beginning of that long, long trek to Oregon Country. So far, the way had been through tall green grass and abundant flowers along the south bank of the North Platte. It had been easy going, made more enjoyable by occasional link-ups with other trains also on the way west. Frequently, other trains rolled companionably with them, the assorted stock mewling contentedly to each other as if chatting about the home barnyards they had left behind. When the trains reached the South Platte, the combined herds totaled more than two hundred head, and the number of wagons doubled. At the junction of the two rivers, they found a perfect campsite: a large grassy field nearly surrounded by cottonwood trees. Feed for the stock and firewood for the people was readily at hand. Or hoof.

The wagons were circled in recommended fashion to corral the stock for the night. The animals were first turned loose to feed until sunset, at which time they were brought into the circle and tethered to stakes set about the camp. Mothers unloaded food and utensils after keeping their sons from underfoot by dispatching them to gather wood. Each family had its own fire and prepared meals in its own fashion. The men did manly things like checking the wagon wheels to ensure themselves that those necessary items were still attached to the wagons as they should be.

About the time the smell of cooking had begun to attract the attention of the men and boys, gathering them closely about the aromas of the outdoor kitchens, the great herd of animals trapped in their circular corral began such a loud baying and prancing about that spoons and dishes and heavenly aromas were forgotten.

The first thought by all was that Indians or buffalo or both might be gathering for an attack. But, before any defense could be prepared, the disturbed creatures bundled together and joined in a bellowing stampede that forced aside tongues of wagons not securely fastened down. The men stood hesitantly about, dishes and cutlery in hand, watching the hundreds of animals splash across the shallow waters of the South Platte, to disappear in the gathering darkness.

The stampede would be a catastrophe of the highest order. The men searched frantically, scrambling to fashion torches from branches of the cottonwoods, hastily igniting them from the cooking fires. They scattered in quick pursuit, but it was already too late. Total darkness descended, rendering their feeble lights to little value. For half the night they searched, until they at last struggled empty-handed back to the campfires: muddy, exhausted, disconsolate. Hungry.

The run of bad luck looked endless to Elam. He would have little sleep that night.

> *1846, May 13: President James Polk signs declaration of war against Mexico.*

The stock still had not returned in the coolness of the following morning. The searchers searched on for a full week, with little to show for their labor. At last, after a full week, they gave up, considering that the lost time had become more significant that the missing stock.

The disaster was worse for Elam than many of the others, for he had lost *all* his oxen. Out of absolute necessity, he abandoned one of his wagons and hitched four protesting cows to his remaining wagon. The captain's wagon had suffered the considerable indignity of ordinary cow locomotion.

> *1846, May 19: The Donners and Reeds join a large wagon train captained by Col. William H. Russell at Indian Creek, 100 miles west of Independence, Missouri. Lilburn Boggs, a former Governor of Missouri, is a member of The Russell Party.*

> *1846, May 21: Mormon Elder Jesse C. Little seeks assistance from the federal government for the Mormons fleeing for their lives from mobs in Illinois.*

1846, May 24: Fremont and his men head south to Sutter's Fort, not knowing war has been declared.

1846, May 29: Gillespie returns to Sutter's Fort, then goes to Yerba Buena on Sutter's launch.

1846, June 2: [entry in President Polk's diary]: "Col. Kearny was…authorized to receive into service as volunteers a few hundred of the Mormons who are now on their way to California, with a view to conciliate them, attach them to our country, and prevent them from taking part against us…"

1846, June 7: Lt. Gillespie arrives in Yerba Buena and purchases percussion caps, powder, lead and other supplies.

Although it seemed that the cows complained more frequently, and more loudly, than did the oxen, the long-suffering creatures nevertheless pulled the captain's wagon with every bit as much vigor as had the departed oxen, grateful that the emigrants "drove" the wagons by walking beside them, issuing the commands "gee" for right and "haw" for left.

1846, June 12: The United States reaches a compromise with Britain, setting the Canadian-US border at the 49th parallel…to the middle of

> *the channel which separates the continent from Vancouver's Island; and thence southerly through the middle of the said channel...*

Sprits were still low when the Party reached Jailhouse and Courthouse Rocks. These two monumental companion ranges of detached hills stood some distance to the right of the trail, their near-vertical sides uncluttered by vegetation and looking for the world like part of a distant and ancient city.

Then Chimney Rock hove into view, and the Brown Party was overwhelmed completely. The thin, graceful spire, some two hundred feet in height, rose in the distance from a cone of fine scree as if it had been planted in an enormous haystack by a more enormous hand. This was "Out West," for sure. Eastern eyes strained at the western horizon; eastern brains wondered what might next appear. *Truly, the West was a magic place.*

Even the animals seemed to be thrilled. The ordinary cows pulling Elam's wagon had been doing quite as well as could be expected, but, of all things that could grow wrong, no one had expected the peculiar problem the wagons were having. The dry air of the Plains was shrinking the spokes of the wheels, and much concern was generated that the wheels could collapse entirely. When it was assumed that the train would soon arrive at an American Fur Company Trading Post called Fort John (later, Fort Laramie), Elam announced that he intended to march on ahead of the train to determine if a blacksmith might be available to tighten the wheels, and to ask whether any oxen might be available for purchase at that place. To his surprise, five men announced that they, too, would like to accompany him.

And so the Group of Six marched boldly out ahead of the wagons. Before long, they came upon a trading post with the distinctly un-western name of "Fort Bernard." It turned out not to be a fort at all, but an exceedingly small Hudson's Bay trading post at the intersection of a trail heading southerly to another Hudson's Bay post called "Bent's Fort," on the Arkansas River. Fort Bernard was a major disappointment, consisting merely of a big log room with a massive rock fireplace and a short Frenchman with an indecipherable name. Alas: the place had no blacksmith.

The short Frenchman insisted in excessively halting English that they should continue along the trail to Fort John, which was their preference in any case. Repeatedly, they asked how far away that fort might be, but the language barrier intervened, resolving itself with a furiously waggling French finger pointing generally westward. The Group of Six stumbled on, wondering what their next great surprise might be.

There was indeed a surprise, and it turned out to be an Indian astride an enormous black horse. The Indian wore a singularly hostile expression on a surprisingly handsome face, and he did not speak.

So far, since leaving St. Joseph, the train had had no encounters with the Plains Indians: this was the first. He was quite a good-looking fellow, they decided: in fact, his features not unlike their own. The only distinctly different feature was his facial hair, which looked to be nonexistent. Near simultaneously, the Group of Six raised lifted their hands to their own faces, as if to confirm that beards were indeed there. Although the man's smooth cheeks looked to be somewhat darker than their own, but he wasn't actually colored "red," as they would have supposed the cheeks redskins would be. He wore no elaborate regalia or feather headdress, either. In summation, he presented quite a pleasing picture, although the very large horse was somewhat frightening.

The Group of Six stood as rigidly as their Indian sat, lest any sound or awkward movement might precipitate some dreadful retaliatory reaction.

At last, their Indian spoke. His lips hardly moved. His voice, surprisingly soft for such a potentially fearsome creature, seemed to float effortlessly through the still air to his most attentive audience, although everything he said was totally unintelligible. At last, in order to put an end to this ridiculous and uncomfortable situation, Elam deliberately turned on his heel and strode smartly away, and the rest of his group followed.

So did their Indian.

The Indian stayed with them, riding stoically and comfortably on his beautiful black horse while the Group of Six stumbled and tripped through the rocks and sand and dust, wondering if there might be any more surprises.

After topping a small rise, they encountered the surprise of surprises. Hundreds of mounted Indians on horseback ranged before them: several hundreds, trotting rapidly in their direction. And all of them most certainly were hostile.

Their Indian still casually astride his fine black steed, halted and produced from somewhere a brightly adorned blanket, which he waved over his head like a signal.

The hearts of the Group of Six sank when the advancing troops accelerated to a full gallop.

Captain Elam Brown turned coolly to Mr. Crowly, a young fellow from one of the trains that had joined the Brown Party. He quietly instructed Crowly to run back to the train, to tell the men to form up the wagons into two lines and to have their guns at the ready. Also, he added, tell them to prepare a large bag of tobacco. *And hurry!*

Meanwhile, the Indians had been advancing with such rapidity that it appeared they might actually overrun the Group of (now) Five. With a great show of command, Elam held high both his hands, palms forward, like Moses parting the Red Sea waters. Incredibly, and to Elam's immense relief, the advancing horses skidded to a stop in a great cloud of dust when they were but twenty-five feet away!

Their Indian, who, it must be presumed, was some sort of chief, head feathers or not, casually dismounted from his high horse. Speaking to his forces with great conviction in the same unintelligible language as before, and while pacing rapidly to and fro with his hands waving about like Alexander the Great addressing his army, he caused the massed troops to still. The Group of Five watched with great apprehension. At last, *their* Indian, having finished his speech, turned and marched deliberately toward Elam.

The chief reached out his hand to Elam, who summoned up all the force he could muster and grasped the hand as deliberately as it had been proffered. *Under his breath, Elam again promised to build a church, just as soon as he got to where he was going.*

As if by silent order, eleven other (presumed) chiefs then came forward one by one to present their hands to Elam just as the wagon train creaked up behind him.

Elam then sat on the ground, showing great purpose. He motioned to the chiefs to sit on the ground in a circle before him. To his very great relief, they did exactly that, just as Crowly bounded up with a huge bag of tobacco.

The chief produced a pipe from somewhere, perhaps by Indian magic. When Elam handed him the bag of tobacco, the chief smiled for the first time.

After the pipe had been passed around and duly enjoyed by all the chiefs, Elam motioned that the watching troop of Indians should part their lines that the wagon train might pass through on the trail. This the Indians did at once, and another church was promised.

> *1846, June 14: American settlers capture Mexican General Mariano Vallejo at his "Casa Grande" near Sonoma .*

> *1846, June 15: Rebels raise a crude "Bear Flag" at Sonoma and declare California an independent republic.*

*1846, June 16: US General Stephen
Kearny leaves Fort Leavenworth with a
small army, bound for Santa Fe and
California.*

After the train had passed through the columns of
Indians, it was discovered that they were now close
beside the walls of Fort John, a trading post on high
ground above the Laramie River some two miles from
the Platte. Fort John actually looked like a real fort,
with earthen walls perhaps fifteen feet high
surrounding a yard about one hundred and thirty feet
square. The yard had two entrances; over the principal
entrance rose a square tower complete with loopholes.

Within the enclosure were facilities for laundry,
which pleased the women. The men delighted in the
forge and carpentry shop, where they at once began to
repair the creaking wheels. It was disappointing to
learn, however, that this was merely a fur-trading post,
not a general store where supplies might be
replenished.

The Party encamped close to the North Platte
River, thankful that the unsettling experience had
ended so well. However, it was not yet the end, for
their new-found friends, the hundreds of Indians,
camped uncomfortably close to the wagons.

Some of the Indians became a bit troublesome
during the night, roaming among the wagons,
satisfying their curiosities by helping themselves to
whatever fascinated them, to the extreme discomfort of
the women.

Elam sought out *their* Indian and, by much
pointing and demonstrating, strained to convey his

displeasure. At last, the chief nodded. He clambered aboard a wagon and made a considerable speech to his fellows, who dispersed at once and returned somewhat sheepishly to their own camp. In his severely halting English, a French trader then attempted to explain to Elam that he believed the Indians expected some sort of a tribute in return for the passage of the trains through their territory.

Accordingly, on the next morning, a meal was prepared and laid out on logs near to the Indian encampment. All the Indians were invited to eat, but only the chiefs, numbering eleven, actually partook.

After the feast, the Indians quietly gathered their baggage, dogs and all, then crossed over the river to the north and were not seen again.

Many churches would be built.

Like the Indians, the Brown Party collected their baggage and as silently stole away.

NINE

BRIDGER'S FORT

JUNE-JULY 1846

1846, June 18: Colonel Russell resigns as captain of the Russell Party. Former Missouri governor Lilburn Boggs is elected captain: the Russell Party becomes the Boggs Party.

The Brown Party squeaked and creaked their ailing wagons slowly upward alongside the languid Platte River. The shrinking wheel spokes continued to be a worrisome problem, for no solution was possible without a blacksmith's forge to shrink the steel tires. Wooden wedges were driven between the tires and the wheels to avert disaster, but the wedges tended to wriggle free, often in untenable locations. On occasion, the wheels were removed from the wagon and placed in the river overnight, but that was a most burdensome task and frequently caused the morning departures to be delayed. Although Elam was now much relieved to have the uncomfortable situation with the Indians at Fort John well behind him, he felt that the wheel problem was relatively minor. His role in the loss of Sarah weighed increasingly heavy upon him, a cross that must be borne. Also, he suffered because of Thomas' flight to Oregon, although he had granted approval to that venture. It had been Thomas' right: after all, he was a man, and a man must do a man's things. Because of Sarah's death, Elam was moving again, from one place to another place, and each time he moved, his family grew smaller. He now had only Warren, Margeline, and Lawrence.

That remainder of the family might have been totally decimated by a hostile confrontation with Indians such as nearly occurred back at Fort John. Or the omnipresent "Plains Fever," so incurable and so frightening one didn't even speak of it until confronted with the problem. Only the perpetual cheerfulness of his former neighbors in the train, especially co-captain Isaac and his dear wife Margaret bolstered him, kept him going.

> *1846, June 23: Lieutenant Fremont takes charge at Sonoma and replaces the Bear Flag with the Stars and Stripes. The Bear Flaggers elect Fremont their captain and Gillespie their adjutant. The California Battalion, mustering 224 rifles is organized into four companies.*

> *1846, June 25: Fremont takes command at Sutter's Fort. Sutter is allowed to stay, but has little authority.*

To his everlasting salvation, the bad days intermingled with the good: for the believers, God's world raged on. His people knew the good times would be back. And so it was that, after all the various worries, they came upon a most pleasant campsite beside a cold burbling spring a half-mile from the river.

Abruptly, the luck changed again. Although God's people were delighted with their campsite, God's animals were apparently not so enthused. Just as the day changed from a pleasant evening into a pleasant night, the cattle decided they liked life better back at Fort John. First, they began a mournful bellowing, then took it upon themselves to stampede a second time. Back they streamed, along the way they had come. Their animal minds were, perhaps, a bit confused, for after thundering a short way back toward Fort John, they suddenly made a sharp turn to the left and splashed into the river, stopping to graze on a brushy island some half mile from the river bank.

Then the good returned. Two nimble young men, George Stillwell and George Marsh, at once flung off all their clothing and heroically plunged into the cold water. In their "nature's garb," they chased about the brushy island until they had rounded up the disobedient creatures at the upper end of the island. To the rousing sound of grateful cheers, the men had all the unruly cattle back in camp before midnight.

> *1846, June 27: Boggs Party arrives at Fort John, meeting Lansford Hastings, author of The Emigrants' Guide. Hastings recommends an alternate route to Oregon Country, to be later called "The Hastings Cut-Off." An experienced frontiersman named James Clyman, who happened to be at the*

*Fort, strongly advises them not to take
the cut-off.*

On the following day, the Brown Party continued
westerly along the south bank of the Platte, then
followed the trail through a dusty, shrub-covered area
land with small isolated pools of alkali-tasting water.
The dust problem became severe. The July temperature
was so great that the poor animals lunged at the pools,
failing to understand why they were denied an
opportunity to drink from the water holes. More of the
cattle simply lay down on the broiling sand and refused
to go on.

Following two hot, dusty days of torment, they
came upon a clear, cold spring in a mile-long valley of
green grass: a heavenly place called "Willow Springs."
All the creatures, certainly including the human ones,
thankfully sank into the cool delicious depths. After a
glorious day and night, they set off again, much
refreshed, to delightfully discover a clear mountain
stream called the Sweetwater; then an enormous huge
mass of granite they knew to be called "Independence
Rock." Propitiously, this was on the third day of July.
They were right on Lansford Hastings' schedule.

Elam was so well-pleased with his long run of
good luck that he patriotically declared they would
camp beside the famous rock through Independence
Day, and even the day after. The huge rock, looking
somewhat like a gigantic turtle, had such a smooth
surface that it shone in the sun. Earlier voyagers had
painted their names and dates on the rock to tell others
that might follow that others had gone before them.
The *graffiti* wasn't actually paint, for the taggers

hadn't brought paint along: it was really gunpowder mixed with grease. The grease was animal fat scooped from tar buckets that hung on the rear axles of the wagons, and was used to lubricate the wheels. The boys (and some of the men) scrambled like crabs up the rock to leave behind their legacy, each trying to outdo the others by painting their names higher than the others. (John Allen, brother of Elizabeth Jones, was reported to be the victor.)

It was well they enjoyed their holiday, for the departure from the Rock signaled the beginning of an extended period of sickness for many. Warren Brown was probably the first. He had, in fact, begun to succumb even before their arrival at the Rock, about the time the Party turned from the Platte into the dusty basin of the pools of alkali water.

Like the others, Warren had religiously avoided water in the pools. Still, even the water they had brought with them from Willow Springs seemed to have turned sour, perhaps because of the heat. *Or, perhaps, for some other reason.* In any case, Warren didn't recover in a few days as some did, which gave Elam another worry to contend with. The sickness turned into a fever, slight at the beginning, although it was noted that he had shrugged off any climbing on the Rock. It was unusual for him to back away from such a challenge, especially when little brother Lawrence teased him so about being afraid of the climb.

1846, July 1: Colonel Stephen W. Kearny dispatches Captain James Allen to the Mormons' Mosquito Creek camp with a request from President Polk to enlist a battalion of 500 volunteers to fight in the Mexican War.

1846, July 2: US Navy Commodore John Sloat's ships Savannah and Levant sail into Monterey Bay.

On the sixth of July, the train left the Rock, having remained there over the Sabbath for their customary day of rest. Then up the Sweetwater through the Devil's Gate , a narrow chute with nearly vertical walls through smooth rock. Again they were pleased that the land had such a western look; especially when they saw in the distance a very noticeable V-shaped rock in the distance known as "Split Rock."

South Pass didn't really look like a mountain pass, for the easy grade was so gentle as to hardly be noticeable. This was the highest point of the entire trip so far, although it didn't appear to be as "mountainous" as most hills in Missouri. More of the Party now began to suffer a bit from "mountain fever." This, they were told, differed from "plains fever," and would right itself upon returning to a lower elevation.

1846, July 7: Assuming war has been declared, Commodore Sloat raises the Stars and Stripes at Monterey.

1846, July9: Commander John B. Montgomery sails the US sloop- of-war Portsmouth into Yerba Buena Cove and raises the American flag.

The wagon wheels suffered more greatly from "Mountain Fever" in the Pass than they had from the dry air of the Plains. The practice of detaching the wheels upon arriving at a campsite at the end of the day's travel, then soaking them overnight in a stream had become impracticable because of the dearth of streams. In any event, detaching and re-attaching had become so cumbersome and time-consuming that, under cover of darkness, the men resorted to a natural, alternate method.

> *1846, July 11: Boggs Party arrives at Independence Rock and meets Wales B. Bonney, who has a letter from Lansford W. Hastings which states that he will meet them at Bridger's Fort and lead them on his cut-off southerly of the Great Salt Lake.*

After South Pass, the Brown Party was grateful that the trail led due west to the Green River, although the trickle of water in the river was so slight that the "River" portion of the name was absurd. (Still: all rivers must start someplace, a reasoning they tended to ignore.) But the simple adventure of following *any* watercourse downstream (however slight) instead of upstream was so pleasant that they almost frolicked along. They came upon a most pleasant campground with an ample supply of firewood at the confluence of the Little Sandy Creek, although, like the Green River, they didn't find a lot of creek in the Creek.

1846, July 15: US Navy Commodore Robert Stockton arrives in Monterey to replace Sloat.

1846, July 16: The "Mormon Battalion" is mustered into volunteer service as part of the Army of the West under General Kearny.

Warren had now become noticeably sick. Really, really sick. Deathly sick: his eyes were now sunken in his head, his skin bluish-gray. They kept saying "Mountain Fever," but it wasn't. This sickness was far more serious.

They gave him *Sappingtom's Anti-Fever* pills, like they had done with Sarah. *Calumel,* too, and that hadn't done any good, either. Nothing worked. Margaret came to help, bless her, although she had her hands full with all her children.

Warren needed a doctor. Elam prayed there would be one at Bridger's Fort.

1846, July 19: The Boggs Party arrives at the Little Sandy River Campground. A portion of the Party decides to take the Hastings cut-off: they separate from the main body and become known as The Donner Party by electing George Donner their new captain.

1846, July 19: Fremont and his men go to Monterey and enter the Navy.

Finally, the Brown Party rounded a curve in the trail and had their first sighting of Bridger's Fort: two miserable-looking sod-roofed log cabins within a frail wood fence that looked like it would fall over any minute. Elam's heart sank. *There would be no doctor here.*

The proprietor, none other than Jim Bridger himself, turned out to be an affable illiterate who did little to instill confidence in any healing qualities of Bridger's Fort. An amusing teller of tall tales, his favorite story was about a place where petrified birds sat in petrified trees singing petrified songs.

A former trapper and so-called mountain-man, he had determined that running a store along the emigrant trail was a better way of making a living than scrambling across snowy mountains to trap a rapidly diminishing supply of fur-bearing animals. He located a good spot beside a small stream and convinced a French-Spaniard named Louis Vasquez to partner with him. They formed the "Rocky Mountain Fur Company" to establish an American firm to compete with the British "Hudson's Bay Company," and they were in business.

They built two log cabins there: one for Bridger, his Indian wife and three children, and the other for the store and quarters for Louis Vasquez. They didn't have much in the way of goods for the store, but they had a forge and anvil and a small supply of iron, for Jim Bridger was well aware of the problem with shrinking wagon wheels.

Still: there was no doctor. Elam walked his feeble son into the store with the blacksmith shop and lay him down on the sleeping pad of Louis Vasquez, because there was no place else.

> *1846, July 23: The California Battalion is officially authorized under Commodore Robert F. Stockton of the U.S. Navy. John Fremont is given the (brevet) rank of Lieutenant Colonel, with U.S. Marine Lieutenant Archibald Gillespie, second in command, promoted to major.*

The Brown Party remained at Bridger's Fort nine days, during which time all of the deficient wagon wheels were repaired. During that same interval of time, Warren, closely attended by Margaret Allen and fed all of the useless mendicants available, showed no improvement. Her own son David Allen suddenly was also struck down, and it became uncomfortably apparent that there might be some unknown *miasma* in the dry air of Bridger's Fort. The Party became understandingly anxious to move on.

Elam considered the possibility of remaining behind to care for the boys, sending the train ahead under the leadership of co-captain Isaac Allen. However: Margaret and Isaac convinced him that would be a mistake, not only for the other members of the Party, but especially so for Margeline and Lawrence.

Elam was damned if he did and damned if he didn't.

The boys were so sick that moving them meant greater torture. Elam discussed with Bridger the possibility of leaving the two boys until they recovered; at which time, they could join a later train. It was a wrenching decision to make, sounding excessively callous. Still, it might be the better course of action: it was apparent that others in the train were concerned about their own and their family's health.

And what of Margeline and Lawrence?

Bridger acknowledged that it would be possible to leave them behind, but they must stay in the Vasquez house. The Fort was neither a hospital nor a hotel: who would take care of them?

In the end, George Marsh and William Scott volunteered to stay behind to care for Warren and David.

But there would be a cost, of course.

Elam dug deep into his purse and handed over a hundred and fifty dollars for room and board from his thinning purse.

The Brown Party, what was left of it, departed Bridger's Fort on the morning of July 27, 1846.

> *1846, July 29: Lt. Col. J.C. Fremont's California Battalion takes possession of San Diego.*

TEN

FORT HALL

JULY-AUGUST 1846

1846, July 28: Donner Party arrives at Bridger's Fort. Hastings has already left to lead the Harlan-Young Party on the Hastings Cut-off.

The Brown Party headed north from Bridger's Fort in near silence save an occasional creak of leather, the quiet rasping breath of an ox, a clang or two of tar buckets. Even the cattle were still, unusual for them. The banter of old had gone. No longer were heard the songs to quiet the cattle: perhaps they no longer needed that. How long had it been since they had sung? *Save your breath for the hills,* it was said. *The next one is steeper than it looks.*

The interminable trail wound on. And on. And on. A lifetime ago, they had crossed the Missouri back at St. Joe. Way-back at St. Joe. That was before their feet were so sore, their boots so worn, their scalps and beards not yet so itchy. There were places the mosquitos and nits and whatever else hadn't yet daggered.

In another lifetime, if they were lucky, they'd find themselves at the end of the trail, the glorious end. How many more long miserable days would it be before they arrived at that marvelous place, the end of the trail? Yesterday was no different than tomorrow would be. In the beginning, there was a time when a turn of the path or the top of a hill meant pent-up excitement for that which lay ahead and hadn't been seen before. The thrill of new discoveries of the West had gone, trampled into the dust somewhere behind, never to be seen again. It turned out that the trail was a circle without beginning, without end. There would be no more Courthouse Rocks or Chimney Rocks. Only the trail. And the mountains to climb. But mountains were mountains, no longer scenery. When you've seen one…

The motion slowed. What was the rush? Ahead, only the next campsite waited. Unpack the necessaries for survival: it must all be packed up again tomorrow. Search for a new scrap of leather to cover yesterday's hole in the sole of a shoe. Be sure to choke in the campfire's smoke, where the no-see-ems feared to tread.

Even the Great Elam Brown, that indomitable solid rock of a man, had begun to flag. The whole idea was his, after all. It was he who gathered together the group, proudly showed the maps. Fremont's book. Hasting's book. Told how the government promised to give free land, just for going there. *He hadn't told about the dust, the hunger, the thirst, the no-see-ems…*

Elam had his regrets too, poor soul. It was his decision to leave his son behind at Bridger's Fort, that stinking, ramshackle barnyard. The son he'd probably never see again. Why hadn't Warren simply be allowed to ride along in the wagon, un-sprung or not? Sure, it would have been uncomfortable. But…wasn't it uncomfortable at Bridger's Barnyard, too? Other members of the train were sick and rode in the wagons.

At least a dozen were sick...deathly sick. But no one had died. Not so far, they hadn't. *Even if it looked like they were a death's door...*

After all: Co-captain Isaac had the same problem. String-bean (as the young boys called him behind his back) had left son David at Bridger, hadn't he? String-bean didn't look so well himself, although no one had said it yet. Not even Margaret. Then, too: they'd left George Marsh and William Scott behind as well, to take care of Warren and David. Two more lost, although it must be said they, brave souls, had volunteered.

> *1846, July 30: Sam Brannan sails into San Francisco Bay with more than two hundred Mormons, doubling the population of Yerba Buena.*

Maybe Mr. Jones should have stayed behind, as well. He looked bad when they still were back at the so-called fort of Bridger, but he never would admit that anything was wrong with him. Lately, he had been so sick that he couldn't drive his wagon anymore. Mary had to take over, and did a good job, too, although that the oxen didn't recognize her female voice right away: they often preferred to pay more attention to their own devices and sometimes strayed off in the wrong direction...or maybe had simply decided to head back home.

Other oxen must have been having the same problem, for Mr. Jones wasn't the only one that was sick. It was reported that, at one point, nine wagons were being driven by wives of sick husbands. It began to look like the train might have passed through a pocket of poison gas like the *miasma* back at the Platte.

> *1846, July 31: The Donner Party, now numbering seventy-four people in twenty wagons, departs Bridger's Fort.*

> *1846, August 1: Mormon Battalion arrives Fort Leavenworth and is organized into a combat group.*

Now so weakened by sickness, the Brown Party trudged solemnly north and west over a vast steep range of enormous black rocks and volcanic hills, further worrying the travelers. Strangely, they found numerous oyster shells, some as large as a man's hand, scattered along the trail. *How could that be, so far from the sea?* Mothers fearfully cautioned the children to give the shells a wide birth. *Who knew what diseases they might harbor?*

The hostile shell-speckled black volcanic wilderness continued for some twenty-five miles through low valleys and sharp ridgelines. To the north rose high ranges of mountains covered with snow, worrisome in itself, for both Fremont and Hastings had cautioned about the need to arrive in Oregon Country before snow fell on the mountains...

In time, perhaps because of numerous whispered prayers, the landscape changed. The big black rocks, the sea sells, were left behind. The terrain became lively and interesting, sometimes beautiful. Tall yellowing aspen and green pines began to frame cold clear-water creeks that bubbled with darting trout.

Nine women driving wagons told another story.
Nine women that urged their oxen to slog just a bit.

All at once, a beautiful valley far below the hills was sighted; the Valley of the Bear River. After descending the steep slopes to the valley, they found themselves in luxuriant green grass threaded by more clear cold-water streams, teeming with more trout. Wildfowl was everywhere: ducks, geese, plovers. Then a most welcome sighting: elk, deer, wild goat. Close at hand beside the trail: berry bushes heavy with ripe fruit. *Prayers were answered.*

If the plethora of the valley were not enough to lift sagging spirits, new wonders of the West appeared that might have rivaled such distant romantic "Back East" recollections as Chimney Rock and Scott's Bluff.

It was Soda Springs that turned out to be the most pleasant surprise possible. Soda Springs was more than, simply, "springs." Much more. Geysers and carbonated springs sprang up out of the ground for miles around. Effervescent springs misted the air, to catch rainbows in the sun. From the earth high mounds rose several feet, coursing water in every direction.

As if that display were not enough, "Steamboat Spring" added further drama, chugging and puffing. *But it paid to be cautious, it was soon learned: boiling water was sometimes hurled a hundred feet or more into the air.*

It was a heavenly place to camp. They would rest here for several days. *Fremont and Hastings could worry about snow in the mountains all by themselves.*

They relaxed and refreshed themselves. They washed a thousand miles of dust and grit from their eyes and their clothing in the marvelous hot water. The poor, miserable patients suffering in the wagons were carried out to behold the wonders of nature, the wonders of a bath.

Even the milling cattle and oxen celebrated, as thrilled as their masters by the bounty: the head-high green grass, the cool streams of water that could be found. There was no need to corral them even: although it was considered, if the corral was far enough removed from the campsite to temper the constant noise of the happy mooing and baying.

Then company arrived. The Party was astonished when Lilburn Boggs and his Party rattled along the trail, for the Boggs Party had been well behind them. It was cheerily explained by Captain Boggs that he had decided to chance the Sublette Cutoff from South Pass, bypassing the long southerly loop to Bridger's Fort.

Elam made a mental note to seriously consider all trail cut-offs in the future.

Lilburn (as the former Missouri governor was now known), upon hearing of the dire sickness of John Jones, most generously supplied Mary with a quantity of *Jayne's Caminative Balsam,* which, he suggested, should be administered. Wonder of wonders: it seemed to work! Whether the remedy was real or psychological may never be known, but John almost immediately proclaimed relief, sat upright for the first time in a week, and maintained that he would like something to eat!

> *1846, August 6: The Donner Party reaches the Weber River and finds a note left by Hastings on a split stick*

*advising them not to go down Weber
canyon.*

Now a bit refreshed by their idyll, the Brown Party
gathered together its belongings and its stock. With
great reluctance, they abandoned the lovely spa to
Lilburn and his group.

The trail headed northwest, away from the
hospitable Bear River. For two days, the Party jolted
along a difficult path through a landscape of harsh
country littered with black lava beds and volcanic
cones. It appeared that the remedies of Lilburn Boggs
had begun to wear off, for the ailing travelers in the
un-sprung wagons resumed their fevered plaints.

*1846, August 8: Fremont marches north
to join Commodore Stockton. Boggs
Party arrives at Ft. Hall, heads for
California.*

The Party at last arrived at the portals of Fort Hall
on the eighth of August, 1846. And impressive portals
they were: this was no ordinary trading post. Standing
on the left bank of the Snake River, and constructed of
adobe blocks ("dobies," in local parlance), the fort had
a fine look of permanence, even if dobies were
disparagingly referred to by unknowing easterners as
nothing more than "mud." In fact, the dobies *were*
mud, albeit *dried* mud. And they were a special sort of
dried mud: *adobe* mud, which so converted into
brick-like hardness by the sun. (Travelers sometimes
might wonder what would occur if the rains came and

dissolved the dobies, but the structure nevertheless appeared to withstand such attacks.)

At the front gate of the formidable fort, an older, courtly gentleman stood beside a very good-looking Indian woman. Captain Richard Grant, this would be: the affable "commander" of the fort, and his wife. When Elam and Isaac approached, side by side, the beautiful woman thrust bundles of fresh onions and lettuce into their arms, which were gratefully accepted.

> *1846, August 11: The Donner Party, now numbering 87 people in 23 wagons, bogs down completely while attempting to chop a road through the rugged Weber Canyon in the Wasatch Mountains.*

ELEVEN

JESSE

1843-1846

The Great Emigration of '43 arrived at Fort Walla Walla on August 27, 1843. For all practical purposes, the wagon train had arrived at the end of the Oregon Trail, although avid Oregonians insisted that Oregon City was the end. Although a trail of sorts continued from Walla Walla, the trail now squeezed between the vertical walls of the roaring Columbia River and the snow-bound slopes of Mt. Hood, in some places narrowing to three feet or fewer, an unrelenting topographical feature disallowing the passage of wagons and overweight horses.

Boats and rafts were available for hire, but the costs were excessive. However: a considerable quantity of driftwood had been thrown up along the shores of both rivers. Fortunately for the Applegates, Lindsay Applegate was a skilled carpenter who had brought along his carpenter tools. Furthermore: should additional tools be required, it happened that Charles Applegate was a skilled blacksmith who had also brought along *his* tools.

It took the brothers two weeks to drag logs into place, saw them into planks, and to build a small fleet of Mackinaw boats; broad-bottomed conveyances patterned after those made by the Indians, each capable of conveying large quantities of goods through shallow rapids.

The wagons, still containing a considerable store of goods that could not be contained in the boats, themselves needed to be left behind. The cattle were traded to Archibald McKinley, chief trader for the Hudson's Bay Company at the fort, for stock to be made available in the Willamette Valley upon their arrival there. (McKinley also agreed to care for the wagons and their contents, should the Applegates ever return.)

The emigrants boarded the boats with a certain amount of trepidation, for, although well-constructed and loaded as lightly as possible, they still might have been a bit overloaded for such a powerful river as the Columbia.

The worst happened on November 6, 1843. One of the boats did indeed swamp, an experience so engraved into Jesse's heart and mind that it would never be forgotten. The tearful words of Jesse's nephew, Jesse A. Applegate, describe the tragedy:

> *"I well remember our start down the river, and how I enjoyed riding in the boat, the movement of which was like a grape vine swing. Shoving out from the Walla Walla canoe landing about the first of November, our little fleet of boats began the voyage down the "Great River of the West." Whirlpools looking like deep basins in the river, the lapping, splashing and rolling of the waves, crested with foam sometimes when the wind was strong, alarmed me for a day or two at the start.*

But I soon recovered from this childish fear...I had not heard anyone complain of hardships or express fear of hardships or dangers to be encountered, and for my part I had come to feel as safe on the water as on land.

We had an Indian pilot. I do not positively remember noticing the pilot before we entered the rapids we were now approaching. At the head of those rapids the river bears from a west course a little northerly, making a gradual curve. As we approached this bend I could hear the sound of the rapids, and presently the boat began to rise and fall and rock side to side. When we began to make the turn I could see breakers ahead extending in broken lines across the river, and the boat began to sweep along at a rapid rate.

Our boat was about 20 yards from the right hand shore, when looking across the river I saw a smaller boat about opposite us near the south bank. The persons in the boat were Alexander McClellan, a man about 70 years old...William Parker, probably twenty-one, and William Doke, about the same age; and three boys: Elisha Applegate, about eleven, and Warren and Edward Applegate, each about nine years old.

The boat now near the south shore, it would seem, should have followed our boat, as the pilot was with us, and this was the dangerous part of the river. But there was little time to consider mistakes or to be troubled about what might be the consequences, for presently there was a wail of anguish, a shriek, and a scene of confusion in our boat that no language can describe. The boat we were watching disappeared and we saw the men and boys struggling in the water.

Father (Lindsay) and Uncle Jesse, seeing their children drowning, were seized with frenzy, and, dropping their oars, sprang from their seats and were about to make a desperate attempt to swim to them. But mother and Aunt Cynthia, in voices that were heard distinctly above the roar of the rushing water, by commands and entreaties brought them to a realization of our own perilous situation, and the madness of trying to teach the other side of the river by swimming."

(It also happened that Lieutenant John Charles Fremont and his government topographical surveying party were at that moment on the east bank of the river, and witnessed the horrific event: unfortunately, they were powerless to offer assistance.)

Jesse's oldest son Edward and Lindsay's son Warren, both nine years old, were gone. For years afterward, Jesse could be heard to say mournfully: "By the elements of fire and water (three-year-old son

Milburn had died years before when his garments caught fire from fireplace sparks) have I lost the pledges of my gratitude for my early benefactors; and this I regard as a bad omen upon my life. I should never have started in the first place. I had everything with which to be satisfied, I was the protector of my family. I should have thought of them."

As the lives of many are subsequently altered by that which has gone before, it will subsequently be seen how the calamity had a vast effect on the fortunes those that follow.

The remaining flotilla arrived at Fort Vancouver without further mishap on December 1, 1843, and were met by Dr. John McLoughlin, Chief Factor of the Hudson's Bay Company. Afterwards, Nineveh Ford of the Brown Party said of Dr. McLoughlin: "We needed supplies and he gave us all we asked for...if we had money to pay for it he accepted, and if we had not, we got it without a word. He was very generous and kind...I have never seen a man who was more noble and generous and high minded..."

Upon learning that Jesse's cattle were to be traded by Archibald McKinley for inferior Spanish stock, McLoughlin sent word to Walla Walla that Jesse's cattle were to be delivered to Fort Vancouver free of cost as soon as it should become expedient. (Deep snow had already closed the difficult Lolo Trail across the face of Mt. Hood.)

Because of his conviction that Oregon should become part of the United States, Jesse had been adamantly opposed to the presence of British-owned

Hudson's Bay Company. However, he was now so moved by the kindness of Dr. McLoughlin, a Canadian, that he now reversed that earlier conviction, and the two of them became lifelong friends.

Apart from the high peaks, Oregon, it appeared, was solid rain, just as Lansford Hastings had said. Conditions were dismal, game was scarce. The Applegates nearly starved: an Indian who had visited in order to beg from them felt so sorry for the children that he divided his supply of dried venison to share with them.

The good Dr. McLoughlin also came to the fore. He determined that he needed a surveyor to stake the lots called "Oregon City" on the ground that Lansford Hastings had laid out on paper. It was incredibly fortunate that a surveyor had fallen into his hands. *And, it could be that the surveyor owed him a favor. Or two!*

Not only that: it also happened that the surveyor had brought along his own *Rittenhouse* compass for the surveying! And, most fortunately, a budding surveyor's assistant named Thomas Brown.

> *1843, December 18: Candelario Valencia, grantee of the Rancho Acalanes, complained to Governor Micheltorena that Juan Bernal, co-grantee with Joaquin Moraga of the Rancho Laguna de los Palos Colorados, (adjacent southerly), had built an adobe by an ojo de agua (spring) on the Rancho Acalanes.*

Judiciously ignoring the complaint about the presumed encroachment, the governor ruled that the agua from the ojo must be shared.

Jesse hadn't come all the way to Oregon Country to be a surveyor. He had gone to all that trouble in order to reset his life, which, he supposed, was exactly why most people went to all that trouble. After completing the survey of Oregon City, he yearned to spend his time on other matters: he loaned his compass and chain to the assistant. This delighted Thomas: he gratefully accepted the equipment, and promised to return it some day. With Jesse's blessing, Thomas rushed off to survey the City of Portland for Messrs. Pettygrove and Lovejoy, for Jesse had turned down that project.

Now with a bit of change in his pocket from the Oregon City job, Jesse began to concern himself about pasturage for the eight hundred head of cattle he had left at Walla Walla, which would be sent by Archibald McKinley after the snow melted sufficiently on the Lolo Trail. He collected the other Applegate brothers, and, following the suggestion of his good friend Dr. McLoughlin, headed down with them to the Willamette River in search of good farmland. That area had not yet been fully settled: there they found three adjoining Sections on Salt Creek that would be available for Donation Land Claims.

*1844, June: Peter Burnett is elected to
The Provisional Legislature of Oregon,
Tuality District, and named to a special
committee charged with the duty of
writing an organic law which purpose
was to create a workable government
and to write both a Constitution and a
Code of Law.*

Half the herd of cattle arrived in the summer of
1844. When Jesse enquired after the missing four
hundred, the drovers merely shrugged, leaving him to
wonder about the possibility of re-thinking the British-
American relationship. Upon asking about the wagons
left at Walla Walla, he was told there were only
wheels, but no wagons. The cozy relationship with the
British had begun to crumble.

But the American side wasn't doing terribly well,
either. Jesse hadn't yet received the balance of monies
owed him for the sale of his Missouri property, and
probably never would. However: he still considered
himself fortunate. He would have half a herd of good
cattle, and eighty acres of good land. He planned to
build a sawmill and a grist mill. Before long, he would
become one of the wealthiest men in Oregon.

At that time, a provisional government was being
organized in Oregon Country, which offered to appoint
him its engineer. However, he refused that position
because he felt the proposed body to be illegitimate.
(Nevertheless, in June, 1845, he was elected as a
delegate to the legislative committee: he stated that he
thought it his duty.)

The legislative committee venture proved to be short-lived: he resigned from the position in August of the same year and returned to his farm.

At the time, Oregon County was yet under the joint American and British control, which continued to exist in uneasy harmony. Adamantly of the opinion that the area should become American, not British, Jesse realized how easy it would be for the British to block American access along the Columbia. Of course, the danger of losing (American) lives by drowning in the treacherous river would be foremost in his mind: *it was necessary to find a safer route for emigrants.* ***American emigrants, of course.***

Jesse wasn't alone: Samuel Barlow was of the same mind. He began a search for a new route around the southerly slope of Mt. Hood on September 24, 1845, but the rain and snow of winter already caught his people before they were able to hack out a road. In the same year, after an entire family had been lost in the Columbia, Stephen Meek proposed an alternate route all from Fort Boise. This route, however, quickly fell into disuse because of the continued sickness of emigrants caused by dangerously impure water.

Finally, in the Spring of 1846, Oregon Provisional Governor George Abernathy lobbied for an exploring party to locate a southern route. A public meeting was held on March 14, 1846 in Salem for the purpose of securing a volunteer exploring party, although the provisional government had "no revenue, nor any means to do anything towards making a road." A group of men under the leadership of General Cornelius Gilliam began the search. One member of the group, Levi Scott, stated: "We had no guide nor leader, and our party was without organization. In starting out we had overlooked the important principal that an organized plan, with a head and leader is essential to the success of almost every undertaking."

> *1846, June 14: A group of pioneer settlers near Sutter's Fort proceed to Sonoma, where they capture General Vallejo, haul down the Mexican flag, raise the "Bear Flag" and proclaim California a Republic.*

> *1846, June 15: The Oregon Treaty with Great Britain is signed, establishing the 49th parallel as the boundary between the United States and the British Northwest territory.*

> *1846, June 16: Fremont directs Vallejo to be imprisoned at Sutter's Fort*

A few days later, after General Gilliam left the group, three more became discouraged, abandoned the enterprise, and headed for home. The rest went on for two more days before deciding to return home. On June 25, 1846, the *Oregon Spectator* wrote in an editorial: "...it will afford us no small gratification, to be able to give the names of the patriotic little band, who inspired the safety and welfare of this country...that they will richly deserve our praise and gratitude..."

Jesse and Lindsay decided enough was enough: it was time for them to step forward. They gathered together a road-hunting expedition of fifteen men, eleven of whom had been on General Gilliam's first exploring party. Jesse was elected captain: Levi Scott and David Goff became lieutenants. Each man had his own packhorse and saddle, making thirty animals to care for and guard every night.

The company, named the "South Road Expedition," adopted a governing strategy called "Committee-of-the-Whole." Although Jesse had been elected Captain, he followed the wishes of the Committee. They headed south on the Hudson's Bay company trail to the Old California trail toward Sacramento, past Grave Creek, down into the Rogue River Valley to present-day Ashland and along Lower Klamath Lake into present-day California, turning northeast toward Tule Lake.

> *1846, July 7: The "California Republic" ends when Commodore John D. Sloat raises the Stars and Stripes at Monterey.*

Continuing east, they traversed around Goose Lake, entered Surprise Valley and High Rock Canyon and the Black Rock Mountains, where they found both hot and cold springs. They split into two parties east of Black Rock, for some declared they should head south to Mary's river. Captain Applegate declared that he was of the opinion that the party should head east: accordingly, he went east with six members while the balance went south.

1846, July 9: Captain John B. Montgomery of the U.S.S. Portsmouth *raises the American flag in* Yerba Buena. [Portsmouth Square, Clay and Kearny streets.]

Captain Applegate, it appeared, had the better sense of direction: his group reached the California Trail and the Humboldt River on the twentieth of July, 1846. Upon the arrival of the remainder of the group, he went off by himself, wrapped up in a blanket in spite of that summer's great heat and lay down in the shade of a sagebrush. In time, he rose, whipped away the blanket and proposed they all kneel down to thank God for their deliverance.

Astounded by the display of serious drama, it is not recorded that the followers complied with the suggestion. It isn't known how many actually wanted to, but resisted because they feared they might be ridiculed by the others. On the other hand, they may have felt that this particular river didn't deserve such devotion.

They might have been right: the stream (if, indeed it should properly even be called a *stream*), would, at first glance, hardly qualify as biblically significant. Rarely forty feet wide at its widest, and thigh-deep at its deepest and a mere three-hundred and fifty miles long, this is one of only a few rivers in the world that goes nowhere. From its beginning in a location called, appropriately, "Wells," it increases in size for perhaps one-half its length, then decreases until it totally disappears in a location called, also appropriately, the "Sink."

Between those two rather indistinct natural devices, the river has been called the "meanest and muddiest, filthy stream, murky and green with ropes of algae waving in its sluggish current." In 1850, Dr. Horace Belknap said of the river's muses: "Her seven devils were cast out, but yours are in you still."

Yet, this most miserable of rivers once provided (before the Interstate) the only road to support traffic from South Pass to California. It provided water (even if poor water), and grass (even if poor grass) through some of the most "God-forsaken, barren and desolate land in North America," according to A.J. McCall.

The explorers turned left and worked their way up the river for three days. Upon reaching the spread-out river in a location called "Little Meadow" [Rye Patch], they looked to the west and could see a pass through a ridge that had the appearance of Black Rock (Desert), through which they had ventured earlier. Levi Scott and William Parker went off to explore. They found water at fifteen miles out [Antelope Spring]: going farther, they discovered more water (Rabbit Hole Spring) all within a day's journey of the river.

They party rested, delighted that they had successfully discovered the southern trail.

1846, August 1: General Vallejo is released from captivity at Sutter's Fort.

The explorers had ridden the road on horseback. Much work was needed to make the trail passable for wagons. Together, they estimated that the services of about thirty strong men would be required to improve the trail. Accordingly, the Company agreed that *if a sufficient number of men were not secured, no one was to be encouraged to use the new road until they had found thirty strong men willing to do the work.*

The crew ran low on food, so Jesse, Moses Harris, Henry Bogus, David Goff and John Owens agreed to go to Fort Hall to obtain supplies, leaving the rest of the Company to begin working on the new road and to direct any travelers that might appear.

The supply group arrived at Fort Hall August 8, 1846. On the very next day, Jesse wrote the following letter to his brother Lindsay:

Dear Brother,

I arrived here yesterday alone and on foot from Willamette Valley at the head of a party to meet the emigration. We left our homes on Willamette the 22d June last to explore a Southern route into that valley from the U.S.—After much labor and suffering we succeeded in our object tho it occupied us so long that a part of the emigrants had passed our place of intersection with the old road (presumably, the California Trail) *before we could possibly reach it.*

The new route follows the California road about 350 miles from here, it then leaves Ogdens or Marys river (or Humboldt River) *and enters Oregon by the way of the Clamet Lakes* (sic) *Rogue River, Umpqua and the head of the Willamette Valley—it shortens the road—avoids the dangers of Snake & Columbia rivers and passes of the Cascade Mts.—there is almost every place plenty of grass and water & every wagon ox or cow may enter Oregon.*

I would give you a more lengthy description of this road if I had time or opportunity but I cannot escape the importunities of the emigrants who are pursuing me into every room of the fort (Hall) *and besieging me with endless questions on all possible subjects—so much am I confused that I scarce know what I have written or wish to write—Suffice to say we fully succeeded in our object tho not a man of us had ever been in the country before—*

I met Larkin Stanley going to California and Oregon who told me you were coming out to Oregon next year, if it is so I am glad to hear it—and gladder still that I have assisted in finding a new route. I would write and wish to write much to you but at present I have no opportunity the emigrants will give me no peace...Jesse Applegate

In spite of the tumultuous masses bombarding Jesse at the fort and his resultant lack of time, on the following day, he did manage to write an open letter to future Oregon emigrants, which he then mailed to the *Western Expositor* in Independence, Missouri: *Gentlemen: The undersigned are happy to inform you that a southern route to the Willamette has just been explored, and a portion of the emigrants of the present year are now on the road. Owing to the unavoidable delay, the exploring party did not arrive at the fork of the road until some of the front companies of emigrants were passed, perhaps eighty or one hundred wagons...The advantage gained to the emigrants by this route is of greatest importance—the distance is considerably shortened, the grass and water plenty...Editors of Missouri, Illinois, and Iowa, friendly to the prosperity of Oregon will please insert the foregoing communication....Jesse Applegate.*

Apparently, Jesse had forgotten about the agreement made with his men that "if they didn't improve the trail sufficiently to permit the passage of wagons, no one was to be encouraged to use the new road."

TWELVE

APPLEGATE'S TRAIL

AUGUST-SEPTEMBER 1846

1846, August 12: The SS Warren, under Commander Hull, arrives in Monterey with the news that war had been declared between the United States and Mexico.

Elam and Isaac stood at Fort Hall's front gate as patiently as they could, still clutching their bundles of onions and lettuce. The gracious Captain Grant, his left arm protectively curled about the shoulders of his beautiful Indian wife, discussed good and bad attributes about several locations where the Brown Party might comfortably camp for a few days.

As the discussion progressed, Elam began to note a familiar-sounding voice from the past. The voice began in a mild tone, then slowly gained intensity until it began to roll like a biblical thunderstorm through the open gate. Sounding like a Methodistic John Wesley preaching to a field of zealous worshippers might have, Elam recognized the penetrating intonations of none other than the surveyor Jesse Applegate. Puzzled by the man's appearance at this remote location, Elam sidled slightly sideways, to get a better look, for Captain Grant blocked his view. Indeed it was Jesse, speaking to a small group as only Jesse might: blaring unnecessarily loud as if shouting directions to a chainman some miles distant. Elam drew away from the accommodating Captain Grant and his captivating wife to saunter innocently through the gate into the fort's interior.

Elam hadn't seen the tall surveyor since the survey of his land in the Platte. *What was he doing here, on the wilds of the Oregon Trail?* Elam edged closer. That it was Jesse Applegate was an absolute certainty: the man, still tall, towered over six feet, his head high above the little congregation as if he stood on a box. The rattle of onion skins indicated that Isaac had entered the fort as well: Jesse's eyes flicked momentarily to the two newcomers with the noisy vegetables, but if he recognized them, he made no sign.

Jesse spoke with great enthusiasm about a new route to Oregon, just discovered. *This new trail,* he accentuated had aplenty of water and aplenty of grass, as if the other did not. Guardedly lowering his voice, he almost whispered that the new trail was shorter than the old. Then, in full dramatic volume: **much shorter.** It became evident that their old friend Jesse Applegate had gained expertise entirely unrelated to surveying.

But even the *suggestion* of a shorter route would not have gone without notice to any that had been on the trail already for a solid three months. Elam recalled the episode at Steamboat Springs, when Lilburn Boggs and his Company, which formerly been traveling well *behind* the Brown Party, had suddenly appeared at the campground well *before* them! And it was because, Lilburn had explained, that they had taken one of the so-called "cut-offs," which permitted him to avoid the long dog-leg down to Bridger's Fort.

If only *they* had not gone to Bridger's Fort, Elam considered. *Warren might still be with the wagon train.*

Jesse, now the accomplished orator, recognized the magic moment when the audience is suddenly in the palm of the speaker's hand. And he sized the advantage: his eloquence ratcheted up a full notch. Like Wesley denouncing the devil, and rolling his eyes, his head and his hands simultaneously, he shouted out that a wagon trail did not *exist* around Mount Hood!

Elam, simultaneously flustered and inflamed, wondered: *Where did this guy learn to demonstrate like this?* Jesse, savoring the moment, didn't relax. He reveled at the dismay on his listeners' faces, then returned to the booming voice technique. *Oh, there was a trail, all right. But it was a* horse *trail, not a wagon trail. In fact, it was barely wide enough for horses!*

The audience gasped.

It was possible to go down the river by boat, he told them. *If you had a boat.* Or, they could go down the river on a raft. *If you built a raft.* He stood waiting, ready to pounce on questions.

After a quiet moment, it was time to drive the point home. In his softest, most condescending tone, he sympathetically explained that these good people assembled here would need to give up their wagons, give up all the good stuff they dragged all the way from Missouri. The cattle? They'd have to sell the cattle, of course. His voice dripped with sympathy: *If...they...can find a buyer.*

The audience sagged. Jesse paused, waiting for the perfect moment.

Then he saved them.

In the most pleasant, warm, comfortable tone possible, he reminded them more about the *new* trail. *Tell 'em. Then tell 'em what you told 'em.* Plenty of water. Plenty of grass. Plenty wide enough for wagons.

The collective sigh of relief was audible.

Then, the *coup de grace:* **The new trail was shorter.**

One member of the audience wasn't hooked.

Mr. Cautious (Elam Brown) wasn't so sure.

Lansford Hastings, in his *Emigrants' Guide to Oregon and California,* hadn't said *anything* about the narrow trail. Or…had he? Written in a typical lawyer's obscure wordy fashion, that wordiness could mean just about anything. Come to think of it, Hastings **might** have written that they **might not** take the wagons all the way. But, if he said it at all, he certainly hadn't said it as Jesse Applegate said it.

If Jesse Applegate was right, the Brown Party was in real trouble…

> *1846, August 13: Commodore Stockton and Lt. Col. Fremont capture Pueblo de Los Angeles without a shot fired. Lt. Archibald Gillespie is appointed military commander of the town: he at once place sit under martial law.*

The Brown Party discussed the matter. At great length, they discussed the matter. For two days they discussed the matter. They collared the good Captain Grant for confirmation of things Jesse had said. They found they could rent boats, but the rental was expensive and the boats were small. Furthermore, the river was dangerous. The narrow trail, oddly named "Lolo," was worse than narrow: it was difficult and dangerous, like the river. The cattle? Out of the question.

This was all very terrible news, on top of the Company's trouble with the Plains Fever, which was taking an ever-larger toll on the Company. Even Isaac, that tough, skinny farmer, had it. Elam eyed the deepening color of his friend's cheeks and saw that it fast taking hold, although steadfastly denied. Isaac's son Andrew had already advanced to such a difficult stage that he rarely poked his head outside the wagon. And Isaac's wife Margaret was failing fast: the Company hadn't seen her outside the wagon for weeks.

The vote was a foregone conclusion.

Applegate's Trail won by a landslide.

The Brown Company rolled south from Fort Hall on the morning of August 15, 1846. Most of the Company did: all but Andrew Allen. He had become so ill during the night that he didn't even *mind* staying behind. Captain Grant's stunning wife promised to take good care of him. He graciously submitted.

The ruts of the Oregon Trail led them along the left bank of the Snake River to its confluence with the northerly flowing Raft River. They camped at the intersection with the California Trail, the last chance to change their minds. After a sleepless night, the absolute final-final decision was made to follow the California Trail for four hundred miles, then turn right on Applegate's Trail to Oregon.

1846, August 17: Stockton receives from Captain Hull, who had arrived on the S.S. Warren, the first official notice of the declaration of war by the United States on Mexico.

When the Brown Party awoke early on the morning of August 17, 1846, the choice was a *fait accompli*. As they were cooking their breakfasts. Jesse Applegate, his road-crew workers and his pack mules loaded with supplies rode up. They halted only momentarily: without bothering to dismount, Jesse announced that a stick would be left as a marker at the turn-off.

Elam must have been greatly relieved to know that they must travel four hundred miles through a vast desert watching for a stick in the sand.

The trail was easy to follow, running along the left bank of the northerly flowing Raft River. After two days, it crossed that small river and climbed over a range of hills through an area so rocky it was called "The City of Rocks." Many of the up-tilted rocks had the appearance of rows of tombstones: a dismal omen for a series of ominous calamities that soon would befall the Company. Some sixty miles later, they entered the "Thousand Spring Valley," recalling for them the pleasant Soda Springs area they had traveled through before arriving at Fort Hall.

1846, August 17: Commodore Robert F. Stockton declares the annexation of California and himself as governor.

1846, August 22: The Donner party, following the advice of Lansford Hastings, enters the Salt Lake Valley. Summer is drawing to a close, and they still have 600 miles to go.

Thomas Adams at last lost his long battle with the misery of the Plains Fever in the Thousand Spring Valley. It was a pleasant place to die, should dying become necessary: they buried him within a circle of rocks that looked as if it might have been arranged especially for him. Thomas left behind his widow, a son, and three daughters, as well as a growing uneasiness by the dozen or so members of the Company in earlier stages of the malady.

After clearing the high rocky ridge, the trail wound downhill some fifty miles to the headwaters of the infamous Humboldt River. This was a brand-new name for a very old river, bestowed when "The Pathfinder" Lieutenant John Fremont chose to honor the Prussian geographer Friedrich Wilhelm Heinrich Alexander von Humboldt. Already suffering from a long succession of names, chief among them Paul's River, Mary's River, St. Mary's River, Swampy River, Barren River, and Ogden's River, it is supposed that the lieutenant must have hoped that the addition of Humboldt's name would clear up the confusion.

Elam recalled *A map of Mexico, Louisiana, and the Missouri Territory, East and West Florida, Georgia, South Carolina & part of the Island of Cuba,* on which map a mysterious lake was shown, which flowed all the way to the Pacific Ocean. Credit for the map was given to John H. Robinson, M.D., although no one was ever able to find the lake or the two rivers. The huge map sold for $15 a copy, and more accurately detailed Florida and Cuba than the way to California.

Descriptions of the multi-named river itself were even more numerous than the names: "murky and green, ropes of algae, water salty, like slippery soap, banks muddy, fetid muck, hot under the scalding sun, foul water, poor grass, god-forsaken and desolate, it finally dies at the Sink, swallowed up by the thirsty land." If Fremont had intended to honor the Prussian, he chose a poor river for the honor.

Those aboard wagons clambered down to join those already afoot on the muddy river bank. Some splashed their faces in the murky water and were surprised to find the water so warm. *There was little to be loved about this river.*

> *Paiute Chief Tri-ki-zo [Truckee] and his brother [Pancho] guide the Imus/Aram Party, 50 people in 12 wagons, to a route along the south side of [Donner] Lake and up [Coldstream] Canyon to a saddle [Roller Pass] between Mt. [Judah] and Mt. [Lincoln] providing passage over the mountains somewhat higher than the trail taken by earlier parties but without the need to dismantle the wagons and carry the pieces up the series of vertical granite steps of [Donner] Pass, some two miles to the north.*

Isaac Allen died beside the river on August 27, 1846. It was a poor location to die, if it could be said that any good ones might exist. No landmarks distinguished the area: not even a noble rock. It could only be said that he died "…between the Snake (river) and the Humboldt (sink)…" Even the name of the place was unprincipled.

> *1846, September 3: Stockton promotes Fremont to Lieutenant Colonel and names him Commandant of the territory.*
>
> *1846, September 4: The Donner Party arrives at Pilot Peak on the west edge of the Great Salt Lake Desert. Food is getting low: the emigrants send Charles Stanton and William McCutchen ahead to Sutter's Fort to bring back supplies.*

The loss of his dear friend set Elam to reflect on himself. He wondered about his responsibility: he had after all, convinced Isaac that Oregon was a better place. Whose fault was it that the sickness had taken him away? How many more would there be? The list, already, had grown long.

First was Sarah. There could be no doubt about the fault as far as Sarah was concerned. He, and only he, had insisted they move to the Platte, over her strenuous objections. The ague *might have taken her away, but it was he who had taken her to the Platte.*

Thomas was second. There was no way of knowing if Thomas was alive or dead, but he was gone, all the same. With that weird lawyer Burnett with two t's in his name. He'd never see Thomas again. Of that, he was certain.

Then, Warren was left behind at Bridger's Fort.

Now, Isaac. The fourth.

Who would be fifth? Margaret, confined to her bed in the wagon? Or dear little Margeline. One was sicker than the other. It mattered little which would be fifth, for the other would be sixth.

Who, for God's sake, was responsible?

Elam stood alone by the side of the miserable river and shook his head. Would he, then, be the seventh? It would be his due, but too late.

It hadn't been easy to manage the ceremony over Isaac. One can only have one best friend. It was even difficult to bury him right in the middle of the trail, so the running of the wagons over his body would keep away the desert creatures.

Then, to pound in the board beside the road with the simple name "Isaac."

Elam hastened the reading, his eye on Margaret and Margeline, clinging together, as if each supported the other on the dusty trail in the steaming heat beside the world's most miserable river. *Just where was he? How did he get there? Why did he get there? How would they get to where they were going?*

The first handful of sand thudded alarmingly loud on the door of the clock. *That was Margaret's wish: that he be buried within his beloved tall case clock.*

He wouldn't need it anymore, she said.

*1846, September 10: The Donner Party
realizes they don't have enough food to
get them to California and send Charles
Stanton and William McCutchen ahead
to Sutter's Fort to request more.*

*1846, September 15: Fremont departs
for the north, leaving Captain Gillespie
in charge of Southern California.*

*1846, September 16: Scouts from the
Imus/Aram Party discover a way over
The Sierra Nevada. The Party becomes
the fourth wagon train to cross the
mountains.*

*1846, September 16: Mexicans in
Southern California revolt against
Gillespie's harsh rule.*

On an extraordinarily hot, dry day, two weeks and two funerals from Fort Hall, they at last found Applegate's stick poked into the sand. It wasn't hard to find, actually, because the horses of Jesse's road crew had turned right from the California trail at that point; it wasn't necessary to be an Indian scout to see the tracks. Wedged into a knife's split at the end of the stick was a scrap of paper: the standard fur-trapper's method for leaving a note.

The hot day had turned into a sweltering one, as if the note had raised the temperature: Elam welcomed the opportunity to call a halt. Although the canvas top on the wagon had been rolled up on each side to allow improved circulation of air, Margeline and Margaret perspired heavily atop their bedrolls in spite of the dryness of the air. Margaret's young son John reported that he frequently crawled into the back of the wagon as often as possible just to brush the dust from his mother's mouth. *Just to see if she still breathed.*

The scribbled message on the paper, difficult to decipher, seemed to say that the next camping place would be fifteen miles away. Upon reaching that place [Burning Man Playa], the note *seemed* to say, further directions would be provided. It sounded a bit like a child's game.

Childish or not, the options were few. Before venturing off, they drove the wagons to be close beside the tepid waters of the river and topped off the water kegs with more of the foul substance from that source river before setting off into the dry iron-hot desert. The day seemed to become even hotter, if that was possible. After traveling the estimated fifteen miles, they arrived at a small, murky puddle of water deep down inside a sandy gorge. It was now noontime: the broiling sun blistered down on them from directly overhead. At the edge of the gorge, they discovered a second message stick poked into the sand beside the puddle (Antelope Spring). The note said that the next watering place was fifteen miles on. And, the note continued, twenty miles beyond that was plenty of both feed *and* water.

At this point, the sun had become so excruciatingly hot that their feet burned through the soles of their boots. The loose cattle surrounded the wet place in the sand, to stomp the tiny puddle entirely out of existence.

The unfortunate oxen, still tethered to the tongues of the wagons, had no opportunity to drink.

Nevertheless, they must press on. The few remaining oxen, eyes rolling in their sockets, tongues hanging from open mouths, staggered with the wretched wagons through the wretched heat for fifteen miles more, to finally halt beside another stick and another damp spot in the sand. This, presumably, would be "Rabbit Hole Spring," little more of a puddle that than Antelope Spring. [Burning-Man]

The message was little better, as well. It said that it was another twenty-eight miles to Black Rock Spring, a place that had both grass *and* water.

Ironically, the Company had once been faced with two routes to Oregon. The first had too much water (Columbia River); the second had none.

But they had chosen the second route, and now round themselves in very desperate straits. To stagger another twenty-eight miles in the furnace heat for the sake of another fading promise was simply out of the question. If water *or* grass did not exist at that point, as had so far been their experience, the stock could not survive.

Nor could the humans. *Certainly, thought Elam, Margaret and Margeline could not.*

What were the choices? They couldn't risk moving ahead. To remain in place was certainly no solution. As difficult as it would be, they knew they must turn around and retrace their steps to the river. At least, they knew they would find water there. Poor water was better than no water. And they knew they would find grass. Poor grass was better than no grass.

What then?

Back-tracking to Fort hall was beyond imagination, there to abandon the wagons and most of the things they had dragged all the way from Missouri. What about the few remaining cattle? Sell at a great loss? Then what? With only the clothes on their backs, ride a raft down the dangerous river? Where others had drowned?

It was four hundred miles back to Fort Hall. To return even to that place would mean a wasted eight hundred miles! *A third of the distance they had traveled from Missouri!*

Mary Jones blurted in the quiet: "Let's go to California,"

> *1846, September 23: Californios under Gen. Flores stage a revolt against the oppressive rule of Lt. Gillespie. The Americans are driven out of town. One American (John Brown) rides to San Francisco to inform Commodore Stockton.*

> *1846, September 30: Lt. Gillespie accepts the Californio's terms of capitulation and removes his forces to San Pedro.*

All probably realized that they were, at that moment, probably closer to California than to Fort Hall.

But they couldn't go to California! California wasn't even a part of the United States!

There would be no free land for them in California!

Still, they *could* go to California. It might be possible to go to Oregon from California. Cross the high mountains now. On to Oregon in the Spring, maybe.

The key word, after all, was "survival."

They couldn't survive in the miserable place where they stood. And they couldn't go to Fort Hall.

So they ate their supper while they considered their plight.

Damned if they do and damned if they don't.

So when the marvelous relief of the coolness of evening fell about them, they turned the wagons around and began the solemn trek back to the shores of the Humboldt.

They arrived at the nondescript shore of the most miserable river in the whole wide world at one o'clock in the morning, and when they did, the mournful oxen blithely ignored any and all commands and forged straight ahead right into the water, dragging the wagons behind them.

> *1846, September 25: Monterrey, Mexico captured by U.S. forces under General Zachery Taylor after a four-day engagement.*

Two days later, after the broiling trials of the so-called "Forty-Mile-Desert," God at last saw fit to provide a blessed reprieve to the weary travelers by placing in their path a very clear, very cold, fast-flowing river. It came from the west, this very marvelous river, which was the direction they wanted to go. Upstream meant climbing, which was the other direction they needed to go over the high mountains that surely, they thought must be near. At last, fortune had turned in their favor. A great change came over their spirits. They traveled up the river, crossing an re-crossing again and again to avoid the many huge boulders. Soon they arrived at a cool green meadow beside the river. There, on September 30, 1846, they happily encamped at the urging of the women: one among them was about to give birth.

Little Elizabeth Jane Allen was born to Betsy Allen on that happy day in the cool green meadow. But the joy quickly quieted, for the mother failed to survive. The new baby girl's father, if indeed he were still alive on his sickbed back at Fort Hall, would have had no knowledge of the joy or the sorrow in his family.

THIRTEEN

[ROLLER PASS]

OCTOBER, 1846

A hundred eighty million years ago, give or take a millennium or two, a seduction called the *Nevadan orogeny* began the first step in the construction of the *Sierra Nevada* mountain range. An oceanic crust along the western edge of North America then dove beneath the continent; the friction of this movement generating great heat, melting the mantle on the down-going plate, allowing magma to rise through the continental crust. An arc of extrusive volcanoes commenced violent eruptions, giving rise to the range of new mountains. (The range is *still* rising, according to those who keep track of such things.)

Sixty million years of relative calm come and go. Then the famous *Farallon Plate* slammed into the continent at that same western edge of North America. The *Plate* ground into the shaky land mass with such force that it penetrated some hundred and fifty miles before rearing upward upon colliding with the arc of (now cool) extrusive volcanoes waiting around since the *Nevadan orogeny.*

When the *Plate* reared up, it stuck in that position, forming a near-vertical eastern wall thousands of feet high, leaving the nascent western portion near sea-level. Had an observer been watching from the moon (the *new* moon, of course), he would have thought an enormous trapdoor had partially opened toward the east, hinging toward the west.

The Maker hadn't finished. A mere four million years ago, during the *Early Cenozoic Era,* giant volcanic cauldrons far below the surface blew their shattered lids to spread boiling granite over the newly created mess. It looked like hell for a very long time, but, after the granite cooled, the new surface shone in the sun like icing on a cake.

And so the early settlers named the mountains the *Sierra Nevada,* the Snowy Range.

["As fine a range of mountains as ever graced a ski slope," Mark Twain might have pre-paraphrased.]

Elam wouldn't have known anything about all those grand theories, and wouldn't have believed such clap-trap anyway. He was, after all, a God-fearing man who accepted the less-complex story from *Genesis:* "in the beginning God made the heaven and the earth."

As simple as that.

That's all anyone needed to know about the subject.

No more need be said.

> *1846, October 1: Joseph Aram and John Kearney of the Imus/Aram Party ride into Johnson's Ranch on the Bear River.*

They wended their way westward along [Truckie's] river from the soft green meadow, crossing one side to the other many times (twenty-seven times, some said) to avoid the larger boulders. They traveled along the top of the riverbank whenever possible; but when the boulders were more numerous on that higher ground, they reverted to the river itself, struggling upstream against the tireless current.

The river flowed from the west, away from the great mountains where they knew California to be, uphill and in the right direction. Soon, the river changed course, flowing now from the southwest, not the direction they wanted to go.

From time to time they found occasional ruts of wagon wheels along the river, giving them hope, even if the direction was sometimes wrong;; they told themselves that rivers occasionally wander.

The wheel tracks generally followed the river, helping to restore their confidence, knowing that others had gone this way before them, and not too long before. They wondered who made the tracks, and where they might go.

The cool air and delightful scenery encouraged the Company to take on a happier attitude about nearly everything. Suddenly, it seemed that they had left behind the disastrous sicknesses, perhaps because of the clear cold water they not only waded in but also drank in such satisfying quantities. Even Margaret appeared from time to time, on foot outside the Allen wagon. She appeared to be apprehensive about walking on the rocky terrain, but the sight of her on the outside of the wagon raised everyone's spirits.

The Company was always thankful when the river flowed from due west, for that direction led uphill and in the right direction. They cheered each time the line of high mountains became visible in the hazy distance. In a great multiplication of benefits, the Lord chose to set adrift a fleet of clouds, which, although they partially obscured the welcome range of mountains, spattered raindrops upon them, delighting the outstretched tongues of children and adults alike.

In time, however, the river began a disconcerting curve to the south, paralleling their course to the line of mountains. Anxiety grew: even the oxen seemed to slow their pace. Elam called a halt. It was time, he reckoned, to reconnoiter the route ahead, because they hadn't seen any wagon tracks for some time.

They stopped at a level place where the river intersected with a pleasant stream [Donner Creek] flowing from the northwest beside a low grassy hill. He set off up the hill in hopes it might prove a satisfactory observation point.

Indeed, it was. Firstly, the stream intersecting the river curved to the left soon after passing his hill, to flow from a westerly direction through a lovely forest of gigantic fir trees. And, through the trees, he caught glimpses of a big lake. [Truckie's Lake] The lake water, he could see, was extraordinarily deep blue in color, a deeper, darker blue than he had ever beheld in any body of water. The foot of the high mountain range seemed to rise directly from the western shore of the lake, although that feature was largely obscured by the forest itself.

Looking down, he observed the members of the Company peering up at him. Striding down the hill toward the wagon train, he marveled at the growth of luscious green grass at such a high elevation.

And fell face down into the tall grass while stumbling into a deep wagon wheel rut.

Abandoning the [Truckee] River at that point, they followed the new stream [Donner Creek] because it flowed from the west and along the path of the wheel rut. Almost immediately, they encountered *another* stream [Donner Creek] flowing *directly* from the west. After another mile or so, they turned left without hesitation along yet another creek [Cold Creek], which, although it headed south, followed a very distinct line of wheel ruts.

Darkness and rain descended simultaneously: the Company set up camp because they had suffered enough excitement for the day.

The next day dawned with such dazzling sunshine that even the mules set off with spritely steps, abandoning the Creek because the wagon tracks did. [Railroad: Horseshoe Bend] They traveled westerly for some four miles before coming to a gasping standstill at the foot of an outrageously steep grade.

> *This was the eastern edge of the* Farallon Plate: *the doorway of the Sierra Nevada, left slightly ajar.*

> *1846, October 3: The Imus/Aram Party is greeted at Sutter's Fort by Captain Granville Swift, who seeks volunteers for Fremont's battalion. Upon his acceptance, Joseph Aram is commissioned by Fremont as Captain and instructed to proceed to the Santa Clara Mission, where immigrant families were suffering hardships.*

Elam and some of the men scrambled up the steep slope to the top of the ridge between two high mountains [Mt. Lincoln on the left, Mt. Judah on the right], and were not surprised at what they found. An enormous log lay along the top of the ridge, deeply scarred as if repeatedly torn by very rough files.

Any farmer would be accustomed to such a technique wherever necessary to drag logs up rocky slopes without ruining the chain.

The only remaining problem was to determine how many oxen would be necessary to haul the wagons up the slope, one at a time. The arguing raged on much of the night.

It was at last determined, early in the morning, that it would be safe to each loaded wagon with five yoke (ten oxen), and to place a man at each wagon wheel to push or keep the wagon from tilting sideways

The system worked very well: all wagons were safely on the summit by sunset except an empty one, which was abandoned. [The location was subsequently labeled "Roller Pass," although the log never rolled.]

FOURTEEN

JOHNSON'S RANCH

OCTOBER, 1846

1846, October 10: The Donner Party, struggling along the Humboldt River easterly of the Sink, begins to splinter into separate groups, each group looking out only for themselves.

The shallow pit looked to be about the size of a grave, but no one dared comment on that, probably because of the Indians standing in a circle around the pit. They looked ominous, perhaps because all were in *flagrante delicto,* and the weather seemed a bit cool for that. They wore absolutely nothing, not even the diminutive rabbit skins called *pajales* about their private parts, but no one was courageous enough to comment on that, either.

The Indians may have been engaged in some ancient ritual: an interruption could break the spell, with the result of indescribable consequences. In addition, the naked bodies were spattered everywhere with mud. Speculation as to the reasons ran rife.

It was speculated that perhaps the wagon train had been a bit hasty about coming down the mountain.

And, perhaps, the train should at once head *back up* the mountain.

Margaret was especially nervous: repeatedly, she looked away and back again, but, each time, the Indians were still there. And still naked.

Meanwhile, the Indians didn't move. *Perhaps they were just as embarrassed as the emigrants .Hadn't they been caught playing in the mud like children?*

This, after all, was *California.* "Johnson's Ranch," the ladies of the train had been told, was on the very threshold of California. After traveling thousands of miles through some of the most difficult terrain in the world, mostly on foot to relieve the burden for precious oxen, they had been led to believe that they had at last arrived in California, a wonderful civilized place where women wore soft undergarments and pretty dresses. And the men...well, the men...

Actually, the notion that Johnson's Ranch was the beginning of California was a misconception in the first place. When the Brown Company arrived on that tenth day of October in Eighteen forty-six, California was still the Mexican Province of Alta California. *The members of the Brown Company had unknowingly been in Mexico for some six hundred miles, having entered soon after crossing South Pass. (But they wouldn't have known that: the "Welcome to California" signs hadn't arrived yet.) Johnson's Ranch, nevertheless was the easternmost emigrant settlement in the entire Province, and therefore to mark the actual border of California.*

Fortunately, the "Battle of Johnson's Ranch" was ended before it began. And, by none other than Johnson himself.

A diminutive man in coarse clothing appeared from nowhere and in a coarse voice announced himself to be Bill Johnson, owner of .Johnson's Ranch. At that instant, the naked Indians at once broke their circle and moved into action: some shoveling dirt from the "grave" into wooden hobs, previously gone unnoticed by the Brown party because of their anxiety. The Indians then trooped one by one to a layout of forms on the river bank made of split tree branches tied by thongs. Other Indians then with their bare feet packed and compressed the wet soil into the forms with their bare feet. The Brown Company visibly relaxed. *The Indians were making adobe bricks, called "dobies!" They were naked because, at the end of the workday, a simple plunge into the river would make them all clean again!*

Johnson's Ranch didn't look much like a ranch: just three adobe houses, one on either bank of the Bear River and another under construction on the right bank. Bill spoke very rapidly in short bursts with a most peculiar accent that defied consideration of its origin. As if he himself was aware of the potential confusion, he raucously informed his listeners that he was a native of Boston and had sailed to California via the Sandwich Islands [Hawaii], jumped ship (*Alciope),* and eventually commanded a trading vessel on the Sacramento River, explaining that he and a friend named Sebastian Keyser bought the ranch in 1845. (Bill was able to recite this entire story with but a single inhalation of breath.)

Johnson's explanation raised more questions in Elam's mind than he dared ask. He had planned that the Brown Party might require only a single night's

campsite: he could think of no possible reason to
subject himself to a further diatribe from this most
unlikeable little fellow. In spite of Elam's caution,
during the de-yoking of his oxen, he learned that
Sebastian Keyser was a German who had first met
Johnson at New Helvetia in 1840, that the adobe
buildings had been constructed at the old campsites
used by the Stevens-Murphy Party in 1844, and that
the building across the river was not in Johnson's
Ranch at all, but belonged to one Pierre T. Sicard,
who, unfortunately for him, had been born a
Frenchman.

Elam had already tired of the lop-sided
conversation when Johnson, perhaps understanding the
loss of his tenuous hold on the audience, announced
that he had a whole side of fresh beef that he intended
to roast for supper, and that the entire Brown Party was
invited. The offer more than revitalized the tenor of the
conversation, if it could be called that, for it had been a
very, very long time since any member of the Brown
Party had indulged in such a luxury as roast beef.
Johnson had suddenly become very likeable.

Johnson called on his neighbor Sicard to do the
roasting, and everyone agreed that the French *should*
be able to roast the beef better than anyone else. A
likeable fellow, Sicard produced an armful of stout
sticks and delivered one to each person gathered about
the campfire. Each was expected to do his own
roasting of his chunk of beef! However, all went well,
and afterward, Elam dared draw out the details of
Johnson's story just a wee bit more. (After all:

Hastings had said over and over again that one must be a Mexican with a Mexican's name in order to be permitted to own land in Mexico, and Johnson certainly failed to qualify on any of those counts. Furthermore: one must also be a Catholic, and Johnson didn't look like a Catholic. Not even vaguely.)

Elam, the perpetual farmer, had earlier satisfied himself of the quality of the dirt, finding it as good, or better, than the farmland in Platte County. He casually enquired after the size of the ranch and was told *five leagues.* He nodded as amiably as possible, for he had absolutely no idea how big a league might be, but assumed it to be about an acre.

Johnson obviously recognized Elam's lack of knowledge about the size of a league: all easterners were unfamiliar with that unit of measure. In a quiet, mild voice (for him), Bill casually leaked out that five leagues translated to about twenty thousand acres.

Elam dropped his roasting stick. *It would not have been possible for such a dullard to have accumulated such an immense quantity of land. To a Midwestern farmer such as Elam, a good-sized farm, larger than any Elam had ever owned, would be a full Section of land: six hundred and forty acres. Twenty thousand acres was beyond comprehension. In his mind, Elam lost all interest in the man, dismissing him as a complete nitwit.*

Then the nitwit, acting as if he were about to deliver a *coup de grace,* said he and Sebastian Keyser had paid a mere hundred and fifty dollars for the ranch.

Elam lost all patience, bade his host good night, and wandered off to his wagon.

Elam spent that restless night attempting to mentally calculate the price per acre if the ranch was truly twenty thousand acres and the purchase price had truly been one hundred and fifty dollars. The answer proved incalculable, at least, mentally.

By midnight, he had given up.

But he still couldn't sleep.

> *1846, October 11: Paiute Indians kill 21 of the Donner Party's oxen in the night, steal another 18 and wound several others.*

When at last morning arrived, Elam felt an overpowering need to talk with Sebastian Keyser, to confirm absolutely that Johnson hadn't told the truth about the size of the ranch, the price paid for it. He had found him to be a responsible person, serious and responsible. The honest sort that doesn't play games. But the German was nowhere around. Elam was told that he had gone to New Helvetia for supplies, and would likely be back late on the following afternoon.

For whatever reason, Elam felt an overpowering urge to talk to the man. He made up an excuse about the running gear on his wagon and announced to the assembled Company that it would need repairing before he could proceed. The ranch was, after all, a pleasant place: he had no difficulty in convincing all that they must stay over another day.

Keyser appeared late in the afternoon on the following day, while Elam was still pretending to work on his wagon. Elam asked his pressing questions, to which the German responded willingly in a thick, crusty accent:

A rebellion had begun against Manuel Micheltorena, Governor of Alta California. John Sutter, owner of Sutter's Fort, at once offered to raise an army of volunteers to help the Governor keep his office.

Sutter had a long-time employee named Pablo Gutierrez, a Mexican citizen by birth. Gutierrez, Keyser explained, had previously made an application to the Governor for a land grant of five leagues.

Micheltorena, grateful for the support given him in his time of need, approved various grants of land to his supporters, whoever they might be. Finding the Gutierrez application in the mix, and knowing Pablo to be a loyal employee of John Sutter, the Governor graciously granted approval. The delighted Pablo Gutierrez received his Grant and immediately built a crude shelter on the land, as required.

On occasion, Sutter sometimes used Gutierrez to carry messages to Governor Micheltorena in Monterey. On one such occasion, the rebels captured the messenger, discovered the message in the heel of his boot and executed him as a spy.

Subsequently, Micheltorena was overthrown and expelled, but Sutter retained his power as alcalde. *Ultimately, it became Sutter's responsibility to handle Gutierrez's estate. Pablo's Grant from Micheltorena was sold at auction.*

*To William Johnson and
Sebastian Keyser.
For $150.00.*

Elam could hardly believe his ears, although he felt
he could trust this gentle man, and that it was all the
truth: he understood now how this strange system
worked.

It had become apparent that the laws (and/or
attitude, if the laws no longer existed) didn't reach
beyond the initial Grant of land: a subsequent transfer
of ownership, like that from Gutierrez to a non-citizen
non-Catholic like Johnson could be construed as valid.

There was one thing more: the question of area.

*Yes, Keyser confirmed, five leagues would indeed
equal twenty thousand acres.*

More or less, as the surveyors say.

Elam's mind reeled.

*Back in Missouri, he'd been happy to get a
hundred and sixty acres.*

Imagine! Twenty thousand acres!

For a hundred and fifty dollars!

A whole new world had opened.

*1846, October 12: Warren Brown and
David Allen, having recovered at
Bridger's Fort, join an Oregon-bound
wagon train.*

FIFTEEN

SUTTER'S FORT

OCTOBER 1846

A red-headed whirlwind swooped down on the Brown Party just as the de-yoking of the oxen began, upsetting the order of nearly everything.

"My name's Joe Chiles," the whirlwind announced in a high voice, "and I'll hire *all* of you to work on my *Rancho.*"

Captain Elam Brown, just then bearing the full weight of the tongue of his wagon, nearly dropped the heavy beam back onto the shoulders of the oxen. *Here, he thought, was another non-Mexican claiming ownership of a* Rancho *(my* Rancho).

Lansford Hastings had made it perfectly clear that one must be a Mexican in order to be granted a *Rancho* in California. Was that true? Or had there been a change?

Just two days earlier, on Monday, October the twelfth, Sebastian Keyser stood within a circle of very naked Indians to wave goodbye to the Brown Party, then rolling out of Bill Johnson's Ranch. Elam waved back somewhat perfunctorily, still unable to believe the German and his partner had been able to buy 20,000 acres of prime land for just $150 as they claimed.

The Indians didn't wave, probably because of the date.

The oxen plodded ever dutifully behind their Captain, having neither the time nor inclination to worry about Mr. Keyser and his naked Indians. After all, they had their own work to be done: the drawing of the cursed heavy wagons through a leafy green tunnel called the Bear River Valley.

The wagon train at last burst out of that long cool tunnel at full ox speed into a warm wall of dazzling sunshine. Any command to halt the plodding proved unnecessary: the oxen decided to do that all by themselves, for before them spread the biggest fertile plain that existed anywhere in the world, although they might not have been fully aware of all that at the moment. A big blue sky arched overhead all around the horizon, so precisely meeting the valley floor that it might have been trimmed by a great knife in an almighty hand. And...underfoot...why, underfoot, thick grass grew so tall it actually reached up to tickle their bellies. It has been said that, upon first observing this valley and its plentiful grass, men, women, and oxen exclaimed: *Why, they grow more grass here on accident than we did back home on purpose!* [Wheatland].

After all the gasping had finished, the Company caught a communal breath and set the wagons to plowing through that lovely tall grass like little ships sailing a vast sea.

They pushed through the deep grass, arriving two days later at The Great Hinge of The Great Door. (If any were aware of the events that formed a hundred eighty million years before, no mention was made of it.)

1846, October 13: John Synder is killed by James Reed in a Donner Party fracas near the Humboldt Sink.

Very near to the hinge, John Sutter's fabled fort appeared as in a dream. Remarkably, the place actually *looked* like a fort. Other so-called "forts" proved to be little more than shabby wooden trading posts bearing regal names, where poor supplies were offered for sale at outrageous prices. *This* fort, however, was the image of a western castle: its adobe-brick walls were eighteen feet high and three feet thick. Brass cannons glinted from apertures at the wall corners, just as one should expect for a fort. The indomitable structure stood on a low rise at the left bank of an extraordinarily wide river [American], which provided an extra measure of security should that ever be needed.

The Brown Company lined up along the right bank of the river, worrying just how they might cross such a wide stream. Everyone (including the oxen) joined in raising loud *halloes* to the fort, which attracted no attention whatsoever. They considered the possibility of firing their guns into the air, but the sight of the cannons dissuaded them. At last, they gave up on the *halloeing* and fanned out along the riverbank to search for watercraft: boats, canoes, logs. The search proved futile: the riverbank was as clean as if it had been recently swept by a flood. (And probably was.)

It had been a matter of considerable pride to this point that, all the way over the plains from Missouri, the Party had not required boats or rafts to cross streams. (The single exception was the near-ocean-width Missouri River: that obstacle to pride had been overcome by the bureaucratic technique of a vote, ruling the journey not to have actually begun until *after* that mother of rivers had been crossed. On rafts.)

The record would remain unsullied. The *American,* although of a considerable width (or, perhaps because of it) wasn't as deep as had been assumed. George Stillwell, that staunch savior of the day back at St. John, stepped boldly forward and repeated his earlier performance by stripping off much of his clothing, and, waving to the cheering crowd, walking all the way across, finding that the water reached only to his waist. After that performance, the oxen bravely pulled the wagons across with little difficulty, hardly getting their bellies wet, then, turning to the right along the river's edge a mile or so, they at last discovered a fine tall-grass camping area.

And there, the red-headed stranger struck.

He looked as if he had been made with too many parts; certainly, some were unnecessary. Extra parts and all, *Captain* Joe Chiles rattled his way straight toward Elam, as if recognizing authority when he saw it. The Captain of the Train, accustomed to facing down hordes of hostile Indians, resolutely held his ground.

The single characteristic that saved *Captain* Joe from an otherwise completely undistinguished appearance was a booming stentorian voice, flowing smoothly like the best Kentucky whisky. When he held out that big bony ox-scratching hand to Elam, the luxurious voice tones ballooned to full measure. The Brown Party Captain defensively drew himself up to maximum height and a bit more (but still a good foot short of the stranger) to proudly introduce himself , double emphasis on *Captain.*

If Chiles noticed the sarcasm, he didn't let it bother him. In a tone brimming with Southern hospitality, he let Elam and all the other folks know how pleased he was to see them. Still with Elam's frazzled hand in that multi-freckled grip, Chiles blared like a gregarious preacher on a Sunday morning: *he would hire them. All of them,* he emphasized like a double organ chord, corralling the attention of the entire congregation with a wave of a free hand. *Plenty of work to be done on his mill,* he shouted, *and...HIS RANCHO!*

Elam, suspicions rampant, shook his hand free from the clutch, recalling that Bill Johnson had also talked about "his" *Rancho.* At the time, Elam held his tongue: fresh from the long Missouri trail and still the raw emigrant, it wasn't the time to appear *totally* stupid.

He listened to Chiles rattle on, noting that he avoided saying that *land in California could be conveyed only to Mexicans.* Also, he noted that Chiles shouted that he'd hire *the men,* which must have relieved the women a bit.

And the oxen.

Elam felt no relief: he hadn't walked two thousand miles over mountains and deserts to work on somebody else's farm. Or *Rancho.* Or whatever they wanted to call it. It couldn't be *Chiles' Rancho, anyway.* Or *their* Rancho, even. Or anything similar.

Lansford Hastings had said so. *And Lansford Hastings was a* **lawyer.**

If Chiles noticed Elam's apprehension, he ignored it with the skill of an experienced preacher. *Or lawyer.* Munificently, Chiles added that *he'd pay the men a dollar a day and board for as long as they wanted to stay.* A new quandary arose in Elam's mind: *if any chose to stay with Chiles, the Brown Party would be split into two Parties, in violation of the agreement they'd made back at Weston.*

Chiles continued sermonizing by referring to *his* Rancho. *And this freckled red-headed farmer from Kentucky was no Mexican.*

Hastings had also written that one must also be a Catholic to own land in California. *Chiles didn't look like a Catholic, either. Baptist maybe, but not Catholic.*

The long and the short of it was that the Baptist farmer couldn't own land in California.

It was the law. Mexican law.

Hastings said.

Had this been a real church service, it would now be time for the collection of the offering. Reverend Joe apparently didn't recognize that: he continued with full sermonizing, not softening his voice even a wee bit. He did take a long pause (Elam braced himself, knowing preachers take long pauses when they want to *really, really* make a point.) The Reverend did Elam up proud by moving in for the kill: he *doubled* the impact by changing the subject, *something hustlers do, Elam mused.* The red Kentucky-Baptist face lit up with a smile broad as the valley; the dripping Kentucky voice rose, proclaiming to all within range and some beyond that his *Rancho Catacula was two square leagues!*

That was *big,* he raged, hooking a thumb under his belt for added, hardly necessary emphasis. *And that's why,* he pontificated (apologies to the Pope) more softly, relying on the wriggling thumb for emphasis, *he needed all the good help he could get.* In full unrestrained evangelistic fervor, he held both hands fully overhead.

*The guy was **good.***

Still undaunted, however, Elam kept his guard up. *Size* had returned to the picture. *Leagues again. The Master had ramped up the confusion.*

*Maybe he was a **Southern** Baptist?*

So *Catacula* (whatever a *Catacula was) contained two square leagues! And...just how big were...two... square...leagues?*

Bill Johnson, Elam recalled, had said his *Rancho Johnson* was five leagues. He had also said, at one point or another, it was 20,000 acres: Elam remembered that because the size was so unbelievable. 20,000 acres divided by 5 leagues would be 4,000, so...one square league would be 4,000 acres. So Reverend Joe's *Rancho-with-a-funny-name,* at two leagues, would work out at 8,000 acres!

Imagine! 8,000 acres! The farms back in Missouri, a hundred sixty acres, seemed big back in Missouri. They didn't seem so big in California. *Eight... thousand...acres! Imagine!*

A *man couldn't even farm 8,000 acres.* That's why Chiles needed so much help. Sutter seemed to do all right with his Indians, though. Johnson, too. Maybe Chiles needed more Indians. Or a change in religion.

While Elam had been ruminating, the preacher had been preaching. Elam forced himself to pay closer attention.

His *Rancho,* Father Chiles was saying,… only…cost …him…$5.00. *And that,* he roared through a toothy laugh, *was for the paperwork!*

The crowd, all but Elam, oohed in wonder. *This guy,* he decided, *was a hustler-shyster.* He continued to rattle on, saying more of nothing: "The benefit of working at his *Rancho* for the winter: no war!"

Well, Elam thought: he hadn't seen any sign of a war yet. Was there **really** *a war?* In the Spring, Chiles continued, the congregation could move on to Oregon, where they were headed in the first place. If, he added, **they still wanted to go.**

The confusing day had already dragged on too long. The hour had grown too late. Perhaps the preacher had finally learned that *there was a time to talk, a time to listen.*

He gave a final benediction and, at last, disappeared into the darkness.

Even the way he did **that,** *Elam considered, was impressive.*

Elam lay wide-awake much of the night, his head cluttered with acres and leagues and Oregons and *Cataculas,* whatever *they* were. He must have gone to sleep sometime; when he came awake, the sun was up.

The day wasn't likely to be better than the night. The sun helped a bit, rising with fresh red majesty over the wide river. In fact, the entire eastern sky was red. Back in Missouri, a red sky like meant a storm was on the way. *Would that be true in California ? Or did one need to be Mexican? Catholic?*

He pried himself from the warm blankets and found the minister, up early, a violin in hand. *My God! Does he fiddle as well?*

Elam had no idea of what to say or what to do. Some inner urge *(ecclesiastical prodding, probably)* led him to invite the fiddle-playing *hustler-preacher* to breakfast.

Some would say that when the Reverend accepted the offer, the sky turned blue.

Margeline fulfilled her father's breakfast offering to The Reverend with some good fresh eggs from the fort. The meal tended to be somewhat tense; both struggled with subjects that might lead to direct combat, like staying to work on Chiles' *Rancho.* When the uncomfortable meal had at last ended, Joe casually suggested they walk up to the fort: he would introduce Elam to his *very good* friend Captain Sutter.

Elam accepted at once. The two strolled like old school buddies up the slight rise to the fort. (The "Castle," as Joe called it. Elam was unsure if the reference had been malicious or not. *It's hard to tell, with hustlers.)*

Chiles explained that Sutter's land grant had been named "*New Helvetia*" for his native Switzerland. And that it was *huge: eleven leagues.*

Elam's mind whirred with the mathematics. Eleven leagues times 4,000 was 44,000. The size of the Rancho *would be 44,000 acres!* **Could** *that be? As big as the Vatican in Rome? Maybe bigger? As big as Rome itself?*

Once Joe Chiles had begun talking, it seemed he couldn't stop, which was OK with Elam. In order to avoid conflict, he had created a pact with himself to listen a lot and speak little.

"The Mexican Governor Alvarado," Joe began, "granted the Rancho to Captain Sutter in 1841."

With such an austere beginning now underfoot, Elam had a most difficult time keeping quiet. *Granted" the* Rancho*, not sold the* Rancho*, Elam silently noted.* To himself, he thought: *A* Rancho *the size of Rome, being granted, not sold, had cost* **nothing?** *Not even $5.00 for the paperwork?* The notion was absurd beyond belief, but nothing could be accomplished by pursuing the question: that would only make it become more absurd. He became increasingly anxious to meet the famous Captain Sutter himself. *Find out if Sutter was Mexican.*

> *1846, October15: The Donner Party reaches the Truckee River at Truckee Meadows [Reno]. Charles Stanton arrives with seven mules bearing foodstuffs from Sutter's Fort: all thank God for answering their prayers, as a light snow begins to fall.*

The great wooden doors to the courtyard stood open wide when they arrived at the fort's entrance: no portcullis hung overhead to thwart would-be attackers. Unusual for a castle, Elam mused, recalling the castle humor of Joe Chiles. *No knights in armor. But be careful: watching eyes might follow their every move.* Joe, obviously very well-known in the Kingdom, sailed right on through the gateway without hesitation or hindrance. Elam, less sure, struggled *not* to lift his feet high to avoid trip wires and other mischief.

A series of shed-like structures made of rough-sawn planks clung to the walls around the perimeter, probably housing such royal necessities as shops, storerooms, barracks, gunpowder, cannonballs, and the like. In the courtyard's center, a rather substantial two-storied adobe brick structure stood in the middle: *the castle keep? Where the King went for refuge when all else failed?*

Impatient Joe, well ahead as usual, waited beside an open door, his ever flickering eyes and waving hands urging Elam on.

Within the *Keep,* rough-sawn planks partitioned off various rooms: offices, shops, workrooms, that sort of thing. Yet another door, held ajar by the ever-faithful *Sir Joseph,* invited Elam ahead to a small room with, fortunately, no more doors to hold ajar. A lone figure sat at a table in the light of a single window: this would be the storied Captain John Sutter. *He didn't look Mexican,* Elam thought. *But he didn't quite look like the Lord of the Realm, either.*

Notwithstanding his title, Captain Sutter wasn't the tall, soldierly man that might be imagined: no sword swung at the hip nor spur at the heel. The former Swiss Guard lieutenant and present sovereign of a duchy larger than a continent of countries showed no regal magnificence. Rather, his thinning hair and small pointed mustache would better describe a teller in a small village bank. Standing, he would probably match Elam's height, but not exceed it. Nevertheless. he did hold himself erect even when sitting, as short or military men tend to do. When he spoke, however, the accent belied the appearance. His accent, crisply Swiss, sounded quite at home in these castle-like surroundings. *Definitely not Mexican.*

The two of them took an instant liking to each other. At once, a warm, comfortable chatting began, not about castles and kings, but weather and crops; Captain Sutter especially delighted to discover Elam was a farmer. As the two of them happily enjoyed each other's presence, ever-restless Joe Chiles roamed quietly about, trailing long freckled fiddler's fingers over this and that; nodding supposed approval on this, supposed denial on that. Not long after their arrival, Elam noted from the corner of his eye that the minister had silently slid through the door and disappeared. *Had the meeting with Sutter been a devious device by the Reverend to draw Captain Elam away from his Company while secret negotiations went forward?* Elam dismissed the notion, finding the room itself more intriguing.

Decidedly un-castle-like, the room seemed like he would imagine the office of a mining camp somewhere in central Africa. A pair of crudely-made long tables dominated the room, surrounded by an assortment of un-matched chairs fashioned from small trees and their branches. The furniture mingled somehow with a pleasant aroma of fresh sawdust, creating a distinctly (Swiss mining-camp?) atmosphere.

One table, surely referred to as the "Map Table" so bedecked was it with maps, especially attracted Elam; for maps, reliable or not, were perennially in short supply west of the Platte. Singling out one because of an intriguing configuration, Elam lifted it from the

stack for a closer look and was startled upon finding
the once very familiar name *"Bidwell"* fancifully
transcribed along the top.

Unmindful of other maps and papers skittering to
the floor, he turned the map to face the dim light from
the window and read: *This map is a correct tracing of
the map of Bidwell (Land Surveyor) by Theo. Larkin
Esq. ....*

Land Surveyor! Elam was stunned. *When, he asked
himself, partly aloud, had the young school teacher
become a Land Surveyor?*

He hadn't seen John Bidwell for some five years,
probably. On the Platte, the boy (Elam still thought of
him as "the boy") had gone to St. Louis to purchase
books for the school he proposed opening in Weston.
While he was away, a squatter settled on the land
Bidwell *thought* he had claimed. (The claim was
invalid in any case, because a claimant needed to be at
least twenty-one years old to qualify, and Bidwell
wasn't.) Almost immediately thereafter, John had
helped to organize the "Western Emigration Society"
and headed west in the group entitled the "Bartleson-
Bidwell Party." (Bartleson wouldn't go unless he was
the "Captain.")

Could this be the same *John Bidwell? He had been
so young, after all.*

Indeed it could be, Sutter replied. The Bartleson-
Bidwell Party *(which also included Joe Chiles, by the
way)* arrived at *New Helvetia* just before the fort was
built. Sutter said he liked the "bright young man," *(not
bright enough to read the directions for filing a land
claim, Elam thought)*, hired him, taught him Spanish,
then sent him off to dismantle a fort called Ross on

Bodega Bay, which Sutter had just purchased from the Russians. So pleased was he with Bidwell, he made him the manager of *all* his holdings.

(Perhaps, Elam considered, Bidwell is a bit brighter than he had earlier thought. After all, he had become *a Land Surveyor, hadn't he?)*

Still scrutinizing the map, he traced the *Rio Sacramento* down to a curved place just above the intersection with the *Rio de San Joaquin.* And there, even more unbelievably, was the Rancho *de Bidwell!*

The shock was so great he nearly tore the map, bringing a slight frown to Sutter's face.

Bidwell was neither Mexican *nor* Catholic: of that, Elam was certain. He obviously wasn't clever enough, school teacher or not, to read the qualifications on a land claim. In spite of those shortcomings, he'd not only made his way west, become Sutter's manager and a Land Surveyor...but...*already owned his very own Rancho... that he...had named...for...himself!!*

Totally perplexed, even embarrassed that the "boy" had dared to put himself so far ahead of his elders, *including himself, of course,* Elam searched for more "Bidwell" names on the map. Fortunately for the ego, he found no more. But he *did discover yet another* non-Mexican name even *more* disconcerting: *Rancho de Leidesdorff. That, he thought, was the most non-Mexican name he had ever seen on* any *map.* He dropped into one of the tree-branch chairs and pressed the Lord of the Manor for an explanation.

The one-time Swiss Guardsman explained, in the excruciatingly slow and methodical manner of an army bank teller advising his battalion:

When Mexico won her Declaration of Independence from Spain at Chilpancingo in 1813, the new country was land rich and peso poor. Unable to pay her soldiers, Mexico granted...land... instead... slow, heavy emphasis here.

But...not all the veterans were farmers. Some preferred aguardiente *to dirt. They asked their* camarero [barmen] *to trade drink for land, which the* camarero *did, most willingly. Later, they sold the grants to speculators. Most willingly.*

Elam had heard the same story before. From his father:

October 18, 1780: Continental forces defeat Cornwallis at Yorktown. The empty American treasury had no funds with which to pay her soldiers, so they were paid with land, which the country had aplenty.

Not all the veterans were farmers: many preferred a pint of ale to a plot of land. They traded the land to barmen, who sold them to speculators. And everyone was happy. (At least, reasonably so.)

One of the warrants was for 160 acres, being Lot 24 of the United States Military Lands, Range 17, Township 4, Section 4, State of Ohio. A barman named Colonel Moses in Lenox, Berkshire County, Massachusetts sold it to Colonel Byxbe. And Byxbe sold it to Elam's father.

Elam slumped in the tree limb chair, his mind churning. It was certain the Company would vote to take Chiles up on his offer to winter at his *Rancho* with the funny name: then press on to Oregon in the Spring and make application for 160 acre farms, same as in the Platte. That would be the easy way: work and shelter for the winter, the rest of the trip in good (at least, better) weather.

It would be the smart way for an old man. Like him: forty-nine years old. In 1846, that was old. *In point of fact, he was the oldest man he knew.*

And he was already two years older than his father was when he died.

And what to show for being the oldest man? A creaky old wagon, a promissory note for $1,000. Other than all that, a purse. A nearly empty purse.

If he went to Oregon in the Spring with the rest of them, what would he get: 160 acres, same as in the Platte. Then he could start over. How many times had he started over already? Five, six times? And what did he have? An old wagon and **maybe** *$1,000 from Missouri, if he ever managed to collect it.*

Half-closing his eyelids allowed him to peer at Captain Sutter without his knowing it. He wondered how old Sutter might be. *The funny little mustache, the thinning hair. Probably forty, he'd guess. About the age most folks seem to die.* But Sutter could die on a farm (*Rancho) as* big as a country He had another fort, as well. *How many people owned two forts?*

What about Chiles? Most nervous man he'd ever known. Pretty hard to tell how old he was. But he had his own big farm, and a mill. *So he said. He had so much property he needed to hire the entire Brown Party (Elam included), just to do the work!*

Bill Johnson had a ranch. Didn't even have to pay anything for it. He was smarter: had his own tribe of Indians to do the work.

There was Bidwell. *Don't know how old he'd be. Just a boy, anyway. Maybe thirty. Has his own*

Rancho, **with his own name on it.** *And he sure wasn't Mexican. Imagine an Indian with a name like Bidwell! And what did **he** do? Why, he came right here, right where Elam was sitting this very moment.* **And now he has his own** **Rancho!**

Elam's father had 160 acres back in Ohio. And a tavern. Don't know how much he paid for all that. But he told the story about the war and the military grants: traded to somebody for a glass of ale, he said. And that's how *he* started

They came from all over the world, those emigrants, when the war ended: France. England. Ireland. Germany. You name it: they came from there. Things were tough everywhere.

Now there would be another war. And it would end. Then they'd probably come again, from all over world, right here.

They were all called Americans, no matter where they came from.

And were damned proud of it.

Elam snapped his eyes open. The *King* of the *Castle* still sat at the table, Swiss accent and all, watching him.

"Where," Elam asked, a touch of English-Scottish-Massachusetts-Ohio-Missouri-Illinois- accent in his voice, "might I find this person…Leidesdorff?"

SIXTEEN

SAN JOSE

October-November 1846

1846, October 16: Captain John Charles Fremont puts out a call in Monterey for enlistees in the California Battalion.

The Brown Party, what remained of it, left the fort just after noon on the sixteenth. Three wagons. Only four people: Elam, of course. Margeline. Lawrence. Young Joe Stilwell, by himself, with his wagon.

Elam willed the oxen to plod faster, but they wouldn't. Or couldn't.

They would have been much farther along the trail if they'd left earlier. That, too, was Elam's fault. He had decided, sometime during the long, sleepless night, that the others should leave first, the group going to Chiles' Rancho: the Jones, the Adams, the Allens (a big bunch of them), including old friend Margaret. There were tears on both sides when her wagon pulled out.

The Party had broken up: the majority headed for *Catacula,* the rest to *Yerba Buena.* The breaking-up violated their agreement made back in Missouri that all things would be voted upon. They certainly hadn't voted on splitting up like this: all were aware the splitting was already a foregone conclusion.

Still: if they had agreed not to split, they could now agree to split, couldn't they?

Elam raised the question with great trepidation, and was greatly surprised when his suggestion was roundly endorsed: those wanting to accept Chiles' offer were free to do so. Those that preferred an alternate were also free to do so, and would not be barred from rejoining if the alternate could not be realized.

The so-called *Road to San Joachin* as labeled on Bidwell's map arched southeasterly from the fort around to the right just as John had drawn it. Elam nodded left at the *Rancho de Leidesdorff* [Folsom], unconsciously twitching his shoulders forward, fruitlessly wishing the oxen would hurry.

After traveling long over a flat plain, they camped for the night at a small lake on the *rancho* of Mr. Martin Murphy [Murphys] near the Cosumnes River. First settled by John and Daniel Murphy of the Stephens-Townsend-Murphy Party in 1844), the current Murphy had erected a comfortable house and other outbuildings. Although the grass on the Plain was brown and crisp, that in the bottoms was lush and green. The wheat crop was abundant, and Mr. Murphy kindly offered as much milk and fresh butter as was desired.

> *1846, October 25: Commodore Robert Stockton arrives in San Pedro and proceeds to San Diego to organize an attack on Los Angeles.*

Upon leaving the Murphy *rancho* the next day, the Party crossed the Cosumnes River, then traveled over a level plain covered with good green grass and evergreen oak to the Mokelumne River, where they camped on the southern bank in a pleasant grove of live-oaks. The trail skirted the eastern edge of monstrous area obviously subject to annual inundation, covered with luxuriant grass, wild oats, brilliant yellow flowers and *tulares.* One spot, thickly populated with *tulares* was referred to as "Tuleberg" [Stockton].

> *1846, November 2: Lieutenant Pinkney of the U.S. ship Savannah and sixty men take possession of the Juzgado (Hall of Justice) at San Jose to protect emigrants from a reign of terror by the military freebooter Sanchez.*

Upon reaching the San Joaquin River, the Brown Party camped in a pleasant spot on the eastern bank. [State Landmark #437, Mossdale Crossing County Park, Highway 120.]

> *1846, November 7: Now in deep snow, the Donner Party camps for the winter. The Breens take shelter in an abandoned cabin, against which Louis Keseberg builds a lean-to. William Foster builds a cabin against a boulder.*

The river was probably three hundred feet wide at the ford, but crossing it wasn't a problem, for at this time of year it was only tummy tickling deep; the oxen were delighted. After the crossing, the trail entered a broad plain abundant with deep trails, apparently worn by elk and deer.

After a few miles, the plain ended at the foot of a range of hills bearing northwesterly. At the top of the range [Mountain House], the path wandered back and forth a bit between the hills, finally entering a draw [Altamont Canyon], to arrive at the residence of Mr. Robert Livermore. [3500 Las Positas Rd.]

Mr. Livermore, a native of Springfield, England, first appeared in California at San Pedro early in 1822 aboard the English trading ship *Colonel Young.* Baptized a Catholic in 1823, he married Josefa Higuera Molina in 1838. He and partner Jose Noriega were granted *Rancho Las Positas,* 8,880 acres, by Governor Alvarado in 1839. In the same year, assisted by Jose Maria Amador, he built an adobe house on *Las Positas* Creek.

Almost 9,000 acres. Granted *by the governor. Wherever he went in this California, Elam found it. Again and again*

The tall, square-jawed ex-sailor was known for his hospitality. His house, shaded by two massive oak trees and located directly on the principal trail between *Yerba Buena* and *Neuve Helvetia,* heartily welcomed all passers-by. Elam and his entourage were no exception, delighting in the luxury of beds with mattresses and clean sheets.

The *Senora* Livermore, a beautiful Hispano-American lady, as hospitable as her husband, was a dark brunette with a dark, lustrous eye, long black and glossy hair, and the natural ease and vivacity characteristic of Spanish ladies.

For the evening meal, a table was set out a dazzling white linen tablecloth upon which were placed dishes of stewed beef, *frijoles, tortillas* and tea. Afterward, the host's ample gardens, herds of sheep, and (about) 3,500 head of cattle, were described without a hint of braggadocio.

In the morning, a *carretada* of fossil oyster shells, some measuring eight inches in length and breadth was shown. These, Mr. Livermore explained, were to be crushed and used for lime: they were dug from a hill nearby, where the bones of a gigantic whale had been discovered.

> *1846, November 16: Captain Mervine asks Colonel Fremont to suspend recruiting efforts for the California Battalion: "At present I am much harassed by numerous appointments of irresponsible men, who obey nobody and are more often drunk than sober."*

Upon their departure from the hospitable stay at the Livermore house, the Brown Party traveled some three or four miles over a level plain through immense herds of the Livermore cattle. They soon entered a hilly country covered to the summits with wild oats and bunches of a perennial grass which appeared to remain green through the entire season in spite of the apparent lack of recent rain. Small streams of water, probably fed by springs, flowed through ravines timbered with evergreen oak and smaller trees. Soon, they encountered a wagon road which turned into a narrow street that led them to the Mission of San Jose [43300 Mission Blvd., Fremont].

One story *adobe* buildings, roofless and obviously deserted, lined both sides of the street. At last, they reached the *plaza* before the church, as well as two-story buildings once doubtlessly occupied by *padres* for a flourishing church. These buildings appeared to be in somewhat better repair, but all the doors and windows were closed and locked. No signs of moving life were visible except a forlorn donkey lapping up water from a stone trough.

The adobe block walls of the principal buildings looked to be massive: if protected from the rains, they probably would stand forever. However, decay had already begun, for it was obvious that roof tiles had been removed, for service elsewhere.

Doors stood ajar in several nearby buildings that apparently once served as warehouses. Rude machinery that might have once served to manufacture woolen clothing stood within. Sadly, desolation and filth abounded: one terrible dark room even appeared to have once served as a dungeon.

Secularization had reduced a once thriving complex devoted to the glory of God to a filthy, stinking ruin. The Party lost all will to remain long in such desolation until discovering a garden in which grapevines abounded, bearing good fruit in great abundance. The Party chose to remain the night.

1846, November 20: Patrick Breen of the Donner Party begins a diary.

It was but a short run from the Mission to the *pueblo de San Jose*: only about fifteen miles. The well-worn path ran through deep clover, interspersed periodically with tall mustard stalks sprouting up to ten feet in height, probably caused by recent rains. The first *carreta* was seen: a simple cart fashioned with two wheels sliced from a log some two and a half feet in diameter. The cart itself measured some six feet in length and four in width and was drawn by two yoke of oxen driven by a *vaquero* on horseback. The Party was reminded that they indeed traveled in a foreign country.

Elam fretted about the $1,000 he had due him from the sale of the farm in the Platte, sure he would never be unable to collect the amount.

The *pueblo* itself turned out to be a rather sizeable village of some six or eight hundred inhabitants five or six miles south of an *embarcadero* on a navigable creek that appeared to lead to the Great Bay.

The Party was very surprised to discover a detachment of United States Marines barracked in the former town hall of the *pueblo,* called the *juzgado.* [41 S. Market St., San Jose] Constructed of adobe, the *juzgado* would have once housed the jail, court, and offices of the *comisionado* and *alcalde:* this was to have been the *pueblo's* primary governmental building.

The garrison also included a dozen or so volunteers enlisted from American settlers like themselves under the command of Purser Watmough of the United States sloop-of-war *Portsmouth,* commanded by Captain John Montgomery.

Elam choked back a laugh when the purser waved enlistment papers for the "California Battalion" in his face.

It was no time to play soldier. Already an old man, he would most certainly be much older than everyone else in the contingent. Or platoon. Or whatever foolish name the army might call it.

Perhaps *because* he was already such an old man, on November 21, 1846, he at last seized the purser's papers and signed them. He and Joe Stillwell enlisted for three months as privates in Company C, California Battalion, United States Army, in part because Elam had concluded he needed to be *in* the war in order to satisfy all military obligations, as his own father had. The pay would be twenty-five dollars per month, for which munificence they pledged obedience to the flag, to honorably conduct the revolution *and not to violate the chastity of women.*

And perhaps his entry into the military might grant him an access to **Yerba Buena,** *which, according to John Sutter, was the centerpiece of Leidesdorff's operations.*

A week later, after no training whatsoever, the Brown Party and a few other volunteers set off for the Mission Santa Clara with no determination whatsoever.

> *1846, November 30: The United States sends an army led by General Winfield Scott to Veracruz for an attack on Mexico City.*

SEVENTEEN

BATTLE OF SANTA CLARA

1846-1847

She had slipped proudly into the cove at *Yerba Buena* [San Francisco] on the ninth day of July in 1846 with but a single foresail to give her way, hardly a ripple at her prow. She looked nimble, as a warship should, in the snappy style of the French; equally at home on the battlefield or in the *boudoire*. She wasn't French, though; the Stars and Stripes waved proudly from her fan-tail.

Señor Francisco Sanchez, afoot and alone on the foreshore, watched the single-ship parade with a patriotic heart-tug as a warrior should, though she flew the flag of the invader. There would be no battle on this day, however, for the entire complement of the *Presidio* except the *Commandante* fought beside General Castro somewhere deep in the southland against the very invader now on the *Commandante's* threshold!

Upon Monterey's surrender two days earlier, Commodore of the Pacific John Sloat issued a proclamation that California had become a part of the United States. To support that claim, he ordered Commander John Montgomery to show the flag at the principal settlement of the northern frontier: a village of some 400 souls called by the natives *Yerba Buena*.

In accordance with Sloat's order, Commander Montgomery sailed USS sloop-of-war *Portsmouth* to *Yerba Buena,* where he audaciously dropped anchor in the cove. [Foot of Clay Street.] The astonished villagers stood watching a small squad of sailors and marines issue forth from the ship and march amid the clatter of a single fife and drum to the old custom house, to hoist yet *another* Stars and Stripes on the empty flagpole. [Portsmouth Plaza, Clay & Kearny Streets]

It was said that, upon sighting the *Portsmouth* approaching the harbor, the Mexican flag had been surreptitiously lowered and taken to the Leidesdorff house for safekeeping. It is possible the rumor was true, for flag thieves were again at play the following night. On the next morning, the sun and the Commander simultaneously rose, and again viewed an empty flagpole. The furious Commander Montgomery at once ordered up another flag.

Next night, the flag thieves struck yet again.

Commanders do not take lightly the orders of Commodores. It occurred to Commander Montgomery, now in high dudgeon, that the assignation of a civilian watchdog rather than a military one might better avoid the creation of an impression with the Commodore that the conquest of such a tiny hamlet as *Buena Vista* had failed. Therefore, upon being informed that an American named Charles Weber owned a house and business in nearby San Jose, Montgomery ordered Mr. Weber to be sought out and brought to the ship.

Upon the delivery of the puzzled Weber, Montgomery stood for a quiet moment, sizing the man up. Deciding him a stalwart fellow, the Commander offered a captaincy (Captain of the Flag) if he guarantee the safety of the flag. Weber, much relieved, agreed, and was duly commissioned.

Montgomery had second thoughts at once: perhaps he had been a bit hasty. After all, a captain's rank might sound a bit grand for such a plebian task as guarding a flag. *A rank of sergeant, he might have thought, would be more in keeping with the level of required responsibility.* However, having once granted the commission, an immediate withdrawal would make the earlier effort appear overly compulsive. Montgomery, therefore, added a second responsibility to the first: that of "taking charge of all arms possessed by *Californios* in San Jose and Santa Clara." Weber, beaming, accepted without hesitation.

It would ultimately be recognized that Montgomery's decision nearly lost the war. Even the briefest of spoken words would have made clear that this eager new Captain wasn't American at all; at least, not a *native* American. One might assume that such a name as Charles Weber would indeed be American. However, this particular Charles Weber was born Karl David Weber in Steinwenden, Germany. Upon arriving in California with the Bartleson-Bidwell Party in 1841, he changed the "Karl" to "Charles," perhaps to sound less German. He changed it again to "Carlos Maria Weber," upon finding employment with John Sutter, probably because it sounded more Spanish. Wasting no time, in 1842 he settled in the *pueblo San Jose* and became a business partner with one Guillermo Gulniac, a blacksmith and fur trapper from Hudson, New York, who also was not averse to name-changing. The two of them set up a flouring mill, a bakery, a smithy, a cobbler shop, a soapery, mined salt, and kept horses to while away their spare time. Weber and Gulniac then petitioned Governor Micheltorena for an eleven league (48,747 acre) land grant on the easterly side of the *San Joaquin* river [Stockton]. The *Rancho* was granted January 13, 1844 by the generous Governor, who was unaware that the two had already dissolved their partnership, in 1843. Gulniac sold his half to Weber, who at that time pronounced his name "Carlos," perhaps to delude the Governor into believing him to be Mexican. (Gulniac pronounced his words with such a peculiar accent that Mexican General José Castro once offered him a captaincy in the Mexican army, which offer was refused by Gulniac for unknown reasons.)

Making matters worse, Montgomery *additionally* assigned his new captain the very important task of procuring provisions for the American troops, a *marvelous* opportunity for a wily pseudo-German turned American. Beside himself with delight, Weber at once recruited a party of sixty-five men instead of the ten he had been authorized and magnanimously named his new unit "Weber's Rangers," perhaps to instill in them a proper *compaignon*. (His father, a Lutheran minister back in Steinwenden, once had taken the boy on a holiday to Paris. Thereafter, the youth enjoyed dropping especially favored Parisian recollections into hushed conversations with astonished friends.)

Montgomery had unwittingly failed to note the local *idiolect*. Weber, the recently arrived German, had now been given official authority to obtain beef, horses, and other products from native-tongued

Spaniards or Mexicans in exchange for hastily scribbled receipts in an indecipherable language handed out under color of authority by a strange man who spoke a totally unintelligible language.

It must be considered that Montgomery, only recently arrived in California, had not properly considered (or even been aware) that the combatants themselves might not be what they *appeared* to be; for, as a practical matter, the natives recognized only two nationalities: *Californio and Americano.*

Those who had come from Spain or had descended from those who had were *Californios.* All others were *Americanos,* whether they hailed from England, Holland, Norway, or Russia. (Or even America, for that matter.)

However: the uninformed Captain Montgomery, himself hailing from that mysterious land forever known to Californians as "Back East," might not have recognized the difference.

Besides: Commanders don't listen much to those of a lesser rank, and all on board were.

So it may be seen that the *Californios* were less than pleased when a party of *Americanos* led by a strange person speaking an unfamiliar language that didn't even sound *Americano* descended on their ranchos and cut out the best cattle and horses in return for scraps of paper on which had been inscribed those indecipherable scribblings. Eventually, a number of *Californios* were bold enough to petition Montgomery for Weber's removal. The lofty Commander grandly responded that Captain Weber's behavior was in accord with the proclamations and, therefore, above reproach.

And that...was that.

> *1846, July 23: British Admiral Sir George Francis Seymour sailed into Monterey harbor aboard MHS Collingwood and was greatly dismayed to find an American flag flying over the fort. (It was ironic that the British flag, first hoisted over California by Sir Francis Drake in 1579, had been symbolically lowered by an American descendant named John **Drake** Sloat.)*

Eventually, in accordance with Sloat's July 8 decree that California had already become a part of the United States whether anyone recognized it or not, he decided it was time that actual acts of governance should commence in the Northern District. The first step would be the appointment of an *alcalde,* which title at least reflected the flavor of the local designation for Mayor. Accordingly, on the eighth of August, Captain Montgomery appointed Lieutenant Washington A. Bartlett of the USS *Portsmouth* to the post.

Montgomery had determined that Bartlett should be a perfect choice for the post, as he was well- read in legal matters and fluent in Spanish. However, while leading a foraging expedition of five men (Weber's Rangers notwithstanding) a few months later along the old San Jose Road, a sizeable group of *Californios* suddenly appeared from nowhere and captured the entire party, Spanish-fluent *alcalde* and all, and whisked it away to Señor Francisco Sanchez's *Rancho San Pedro*.

The American Military Might, unprepared for such an underhanded tactic as the holding of hostages, was struck dumb.

> *1846, December 29: Captain John Montgomery is replaced by Captain J.B. Hull as Governor of the Northern District of California.*

> ******

> *1847, January 1: A party of a hundred men and a small cannon depart Yerba Buena for Santa Clara under the command of Marine Captain Ward Marston.*

The rain poured heavily down on Elam and his little flotilla of wagons all the way from San Jose to the clutch of decrepit adobe buildings which, they hoped, might be the *Mision* de Santa Clara. It was wondered why Lansford Hastings had so extolled the sunny weather in California and so lambasted the dreary wetness of Oregon Country, but the group was nevertheless pleased to have at last found a collection of buildings, decrepit or not, that looked religious and must therefore surely be the *Mision.*

They were welcomed by a man wearing an enormous leather hat, perhaps for protection from the rain. He must have expected them, for he stood in the middle of the muddy road and furiously waved the caravan into a grassy field beside the buildings.

The Hat Man closed on them even before the wagons stopped rolling. In spite of its great size, the huge hat nevertheless proved to be too small to completely enclose a mass of unruly hair bent on escape. A ferocious mustache, as wet and scraggly as the hair on his head, concealed much of his upper lip. That portion of his face still visible appeared like that of an arrogant highwayman intent on robbing unsuspecting pilgrims of their worldly goods.

The would-be bandit introduced himself in an extraordinarily loud voice as none other than **"Napoleon Bonaparte Smith,"** which hardly served to calm any apprehension, in spite of a following military-style introduction: **"First Sergeant, Company C, California Battalion, United States Army, Captain Aram commanding."**

Reluctantly, Elam recalled that he, too, was a soldier, recently recruited as a Private into the very same army. *This unkempt, hostile-looking Sergeant would out-rank him by a good bit. Indeed, the fellow might even be his commanding officer!* Not quite sure just how he should handle the situation he found himself in, Elam stiffened his back a bit into a slightly more militaristic pose and wondered if the proper address for a sergeant was "Sir."

Just as he stiffened, Margeline leaned over his right shoulder, appearing from the interior of the wagon as if she might be wondering what all the shouting was about. The rancor in Sergeant Smith's face disappeared at once. *He might have even doffed the absurd hat, if the rain hadn't been coming down so hard. He wasn't, Elam concluded, the sort he'd choose for a son-in-law.*

While Private Elam studied the Sergeant and the Sergeant studied Margeline, an ancient creature clad all in black creaked open an ancient door in the wall of one of the most ancient religious-looking buildings. He staggered to the outside, ignoring the rain pelting down on his totally bald head and held forward a bony hand. He was, he said, Padre José M. del Real.

The Padre grandly ushered them into the crumbling *Mision* as if it were the Vatican itself. After the door had been closed to excommunicate the rain, he explained in an apologetic manner that this was but a wing of a building [500 El Camino Real] that had once served the *major-domo* prior to the secularization of the Missions. Since 1833, he elaborated, Santa Clara has been simply a parish church, although most people still called it a Mision. And probably, he added, they always would.

They stood within a high-ceilinged room some fifteen feet wide, running easterly about a hundred feet along the north wall of the church cemetery. Rain water dripped through numerous holes in the roof, to splash continuously on the stone floor.

The Padre waved to some thirty families huddled in this steamy wet space, who, he explained, were the women and children of the men Colonel Fremont had left behind while he battled the Mexicans in the southland. The odor associated with cholera pervaded the wetness.

These were the folk Elam had volunteered to protect.

The leaky roof, the Padre continued, was only half the problem. He explained that the free-booter Colonel Sanchez, camped a mile away, was moving toward

them with a hundred men. However, he added with a
show of nervous confidence, a good parishioner named
John Laird was even then maintaining a vigil in the
church belfry.

*In actual fact, Francisco Sanchez was much closer
than the Padre realized. He had watched the several
wagons of the Brown Party turn into the field beside
the* Mision, *and watched the Party disappear into the
major-domo building with Padre Real and the sergeant
with the big hat.*

(A Mexican soldier since the transfer of authority
from Spain in 1822, Francisco had been appointed
elector and secretary of the newly organized municipal
government. Promoted to First Lieutenant and assigned
to the *Presidio* of Monterey, he became Captain of the
Militia Company organized for the defense of *Yerba
Buena,* and subsequently named *Commandante* of its
Presidio. In 1839, Governor Juan Alvarado, grateful
for his good service, granted him the 8,926 acre
Rancho San Pedro.) [Pacifica]

Furthermore, the *Mision San Francisco de Asis,* it
was said in the Sanchez family, had been founded by
Francisco's grandfather on June 29, 1776. (History
records the founding by the Juan Bautista de Anza
Expedition, but since grandfather had been a member
of that expedition, it was not considered improper for
his mother to make such a claim: especially after she
named her newborn after the *Mision* itself.*)*

Few were aware that Francisco had once risen to
his feet at a Junta in Monterey convened by General
Castro in 1846 to declare himself *in favor of*
California's annexation to the United States. (General
Vallejo also spoke in favor, but when he found himself

in the minority, he left the meeting, therefore depriving the Junta of a quorum.)

In a letter to Commander Montgomery dated November 5, 1845, Lieutenant Bartlett of the good ship *Portsmouth* had written: "the Sanchez family in its different branches have abundant cattle-and if it shall meet with your approval I can have fifty or one hundred head driven in…and then all that are used can be paid for…" In a second letter, Bartlett wrote"…I found him (Francisco) at home and very friendly indeed…he said he was willing to do all he could…"

> *1847, January 2: General Stockton appoints Colonel Fremont to the post of Military Governor of California.*

Captain Marston, his men, and his small cannon advanced along the road to Santa Clara, keeping a cautious eye on large numbers of *Californios* on horseback hovering at a safe distance. Finally, the frustrated Marston at last fired a few rounds of grape from his field-piece, giving rise to a response of several musket shots from Sanchez. At one point, when Marston's force became mired in crossing a marshy spot, Sanchez made a "charge." (That is, he ventured for a few moments within gunshot range and slightly wounded two *Americanos* before drawing o a position near the *Mision*, with the result that Captain Aram ran out to Marston's aid.)

> *1847, January 3: Captain Maddox arrives Santa Clara from Monterey with fifty men, whereupon Marston and British Consul Forbes go forward to meet with Sanchez.*

Sanchez told Marston and Forbes that he wasn't in arms against the American flag, but that the *Californios* feared for their safety. Marston agreed to relay the grievances to Commander Hull and to observe an armistice while awaiting a reply.

> *1847, January 6: A courier arrives with instructions from Commander Hull: The surrender must be nominally unconditional, but with unofficial assurances, confirmed by prominent citizens: property should be no longer seized without the proper formalities and receipts.*

> *1847, January 8: Sanchez gives up his prisoners and arms. His men retire quietly to their farms. Marston and his men return to* Yerba Buena, *where they receive congratulations for their valor and success.* [State monument at the southeast corner of El Camino Real and Lawrence Station Road.]

On the tenth of January, 1847, First Sergeant Napoleon Bonaparte Smith called his men together to inform them that the Battle of Santa Clara had officially ended, and that the *Americanos* had won. The men of Company C, he said, would be free to go home when their enlistments expired.

The announcement fall on Elam like a wet cloud, for the expiration of his enlistment wouldn't occur until February 21. *Forty-two days hence.*

"Make Haste, As The Time Grows Short," the Reverend Adna Hecox had preached at the funeral of a daughter of Silas Hitchcock on December 15. Wasted and enfeebled himself by sickness, it was said the Methodist Episcopal minister then delivered the first Anglo-American service in California with that title.

But Elam couldn't hasten the day. He sought out his First Sergeant and, upon finding him, realized just how much Napoleon had changed. The great hat was gone entirely. The mass of curly hair on his head, having lost the protective hat, had been neatly trimmed. Even the ferocious mustache was gone.

Elam asked in a faltering voice about the possibility of an early termination of his enlistment, now that the poor souls in the *Mision* would no longer be threatened. Without hesitation, Napoleon doubted that would be possible. However, after learning that the reason was to seek out a land-broker named William Leidesdorff, the sergeant's face broke into a wide smile. He knew the man well, he said, and suggested he make the introduction. Furthermore, he suggested that he might be able to arrange a leave of absence for the two of them to travel to *Yerba Buena*.

Elam was beside himself with delight. *However, he told himself, he could never call the boy "Bony," as Napoleon's friends did.*

The accommodating Sergeant even arranged transportation. Given permission by Captain Aram for leave, the two of them set off the very next day on horseback; Napoleon on a mare belonging to his brother Henry, Elam on one belonging to Napoleon's friend William Mendenhall. Trotting north early in the morning of January 12, on the *Old San Jose* Road [Highway 101] along the western shore of the Bay, Elam casually asked how it was that Napoleon happened to come to California.

Napoleon folded both hands on his saddle-horn and told about the trip west with his brother Henry Clay Smith (Elam wondered at that point if the sergeant's father might have been named George Washington Smith, but dared not ask) and friend Bill Mendenhall from St. Joseph, Michigan in 1845. They met Lansford Hastings (Elam's ears perked up at the mention of his name) in St. Louis, then traveled by steamboat up the Missouri to Independence.

They arrived at Sutter's Fort on Christmas Day and continued to *Yerba Buena*. Low on funds, they were told that work could be had in the redwoods of the *contra costa* [opposite coast] in a place called *San Antonio*. There they met a Frenchman (Napoleon didn't divulge his name) who instructed them in logging and the whip-sawing of lumber. Things went well at first, but they were later confronted by several Spanish [Mexican] soldiers who said they had been sent to drive the *Americanos* from the forest. Returning to Sutter's Fort, they met Captain Aram, who recruited them to help defend *the Mision de Santa Clara*. Napoleon took a deep breath and paused at that point.

His discourse had, apparently, loosened his tongue. After a second deep breath, he ranged on, explaining that he thought the big demand for lumber in *Yerba Buena* was just beginning. The *Alcaldes* of *Yerba Buena,* he said, were permitted to sell lots in the town. Prices varied from $12.50 for a 50-vara lot [one vara equaled 33.3 inches] to $25.00 for a 100-vara lot, plus a recording feet of $3.62 per lot. The *Alcaldes,* he added, also sold unbuildable under-water lots (called "water lots,") for lesser prices. *Elam couldn't imagine why anyone would want to buy lots covered with water.* [The day would come when a tall building would be constructed on one of those lots and gain notoriety as *The Leaning Tower of San Francisco.]*

Elam was markedly unimpressed upon arrival at Y*erba Buena;* the village looked to be little more than a few adobe buildings scattered among a collection shifting sand dunes: more dunes than buildings. Napoleon threaded them along s path through the dunes to a large one-story adobe with an attic and dormer windows. On the front of the building, a large sign announced "Brown's Hotel" [SW corner Clay & Kearny streets.] The ever-knowledgeable Napoleon explained that the building actually belonged to Mr. Leidesdorff, but was leased to an innkeeper named John Henry Brown. Inside was a large dining hall, a barroom, billiard table, and a few rooms downstairs to qualify it as a hotel.

The deskman greeted Napoleon as "Bony," which didn't surprise Elam.

1847, January 13: Lt. Col. Fremont and Gen. Andres Pico sign the Treaty of Cahuenga, an unofficial truce without the backing of either the United States or Mexico, which was nevertheless honored by both the Americanos and the Californios and served to halt the fighting between the two nations.

Following a most adequate breakfast of ham and eggs the next morning, Napoleon led Elam on foot to a very handsome adobe house nestled behind a surprising flower garden, which appeared to be the *only* flower garden in all of *Yerba Buena.* [corner of California and Montgomery] The "cottage," Napoleon unnecessarily explained, was the residence of none other than Mr. Leidesdorff.

The *cottage was* purchased in 1846, said the well-informed Napoleon, from an Irish builder named Robert Ridley. The interior was remarkable but not surprising: embellished with carpets, mirrors, a massive Broadwood piano and a beautiful common-law Russian-Alaskan wife. At one time, Napoleon rattled on, Mr. Leidesdorff had held a reception honoring Commodore Stockton that was so entertaining the Commodore responded with an hour-long speech.

Young Indian servants, probably 10 or 12 years old, escorted them down a long piazza facing the Bay into a large room that also faced the Bay. Standing there alone, as if he had been long awaiting their arrival, stood the Great Man himself.

Mr. Leidesdorff wasn't excessively tall, Elam noted with pleasure; scarcely taller than Elam himself. Arched above his upper lip, a bushy black mustache pointed downward left and right the same time, supported in the center by a small square bush attached just under the middle of the lower lip. Above it all, a pair of flashing black eyes promised no promises.

The mustache and the bush hardly moved when a lilting educated voice from somewhere behind the mustache with, surprisingly, a British accent, welcomed them in tones that suggested it might speak cordially in any language the visitor might choose, should the current one prove inadequate.

And he called Napoleon "Bony." Of course.

Elam felt he had been transported to another time, another place.

Leidesdorff was so like Colonel Byxbe! They even had the same accent!

A low command, barely noticeable in the elegant room, caused the servants to scurry away and disappear; then their host congenially waved his visitors to a large round table circled by three chairs in the center of the big room. Upon seating themselves, that polite British voice asked Elam what his business might be.

Taken aback by the unaccustomed luxury at the end of his long voyage from Missouri, Elam found himself at a loss for words, feeling like a clumsy farm-boy with mud on his boots and sand in his eyes.

He wanted to buy a Rancho, he blurted.

As if by pre-arrangement, the two little servants reappeared at that moment, whispering into the room with fragile tea things on wooden trays. The gracious host leaned comfortably back in his chair as if considering Elam's response while delicate china teacups and tiny teacakes were carefully being distributed on small plates painted with the tiniest of red roses.

Politely waiting until the ceremony of the pouring of the tea had concluded and the little Indians had again disappeared. Then, in the waiting silence, he appeared to mutter *that he just might, by the oddest coincidence,* have knowledge of a most desirable *Rancho.*

Just as Byxbe would have said it.

Leidesdorff ignored the freshly poured tea. The *Rancho,* he said, glancing around the table to ensure himself that his listeners were giving him their fullest attention, was located in the *Contra Costa.* Pausing between pauses, he lifted is glistening teaspoon as if to definitely assure himself that it was faultless before adding a considerable quantity of sugar to his tea. Soundlessly returning the spoon to its place in the saucer, he assured Elam that the *Contra Costa* was, without a doubt, the very finest farming area in all California. *Or anywhere else, for that matter.*

In the ensuing silence, he tasted his tea, then returned his cup precisely into the center of its saucer. He lifted those heavy black eyebrows to full elevation and announced to the waiting world that everyone, present company included, must realize that, because of the present crisis, it had to be understood that it would be necessary to conclude the sale as quickly as possible.

Elam nodded sharply; he couldn't have agreed more.

*1847, January 24: Warren Brown and
David Allen recover from their
sicknesses at Fort Bridger and head for
Oregon Country.*

It was good to be out of the overstuffed tea-house
and astride Mendenhall's horse once again, headed
south to Santa Clara in the cold fresh air that *Yerba
Buena* seemed to have such an abundance of.
But…Elam had so many unanswered questions. Where
was the *Rancho?* How big was it? How much would it
cost? Elam was uncomfortable with Leidesdorff:: the
man was so like Colonel Byxbe. *Still, he man was held
in high esteem by so many.* John Sutter had not only
recommended him, but insisted that this was the person
to whom one must talk if one wanted to purchase land
in California. Even Elam's old school teacher friend
John Bidwell had bought land from Leidesdorff. And,
like him or not, Elam had no alternative. Reverend
Hecox had said it best: *Remember How Short My Time
Is.*

While they rode casually south, Napoleon renewed
his chatter as if the interruption at *Yerba Buena* hadn't
even occurred, explaining that prior to Washington
Bartlett's appointment as *alcalde,* only fifty or sixty
lots had been granted in of *Yerba Buena.* Bartlett
granted sixty more, almost at once. Then running low,
Bartlett hired the Irish surveyor Jasper O'Farrell to
create more lots by expanding the current downtown
from Portsmouth Square.

Right down to the edge of the water.

Even *into* the water.

Napoleon also lightly mentioned that Leidesdorff might sell his house on the hill, "probably," he said, "because of financial difficulties."

This was most disturbing information: that Elam would be proposing an imminent purchase from a man with "financial difficulties." Elam pressed further, but Napoleon simply said he had heard about a squabble between Brown and Leidesdorff over the rent. "They had an oral agreement," he said, "Brown insisted the agreement was for a thousand dollars a year, but Leidsdorff remembered two thousand. Brown left, and Leidesdorff changed the name to 'City Hotel,' but the sign ain't been changed yet...Leidesdorff never did get the other thousand."

When they arrived back at the *Mision,* Elam frantically rummaged through all his possessions to collect whatever scraps of paper he could find; regardless of Leidesdorff's financial condition, there were letters that needed to be written. Each a single sheet of folded paper, they would be posted to each of the Browns and each of the Allens, for it must be presumed they had no knowledge of Elam's whereabouts. Addressed to the most recent location of which Elam was aware, he posted them in the old saddlebag for that purpose nailed to a tree beside the Mision in the hope they'd be carried along by whatever willing travelers might be headed in the general direction of the address shown.

There was no alternative. He had abandoned folks at various locations: they wouldn't otherwise know where he'd gone to. It was time to call them together again.

In his letters, he said that, upon his discharge, he would head for the *San Antonio Redwoods* in California's *Contra Costa;* where, he had been told, work could be found, adding that he had also *located a seller of land who will have a large* Rancho *available for purchase.*

One letter was addressed to Thomas Brown, Surveyor, Portland, Oregon Country; he told Thomas that he was somewhat uncertain about the seller. A letter to Warren at Fort Bridger, although he had no idea if Warren had survived his illness. One to Andrew Allen at Fort Hall, with the same hope. One to Nat Jones at Chiles' Ranch, in which he asked Nat to so advise all others at that location of the contents of this letter.

In each letter, he instructed: *Travel to the little town of Francesca on the Sacramento River. Take Dr. Semple's ferry to Martinez, then the road south through the* Contra Costa *to* San Antonio.

He prayed when he placed the letters in the saddlebag.

Very hard.

> *1847, January 30: Washington A. Bartlett, Alcalde and chief magistrate of Yerba Buena, having heard that the ferryman Semple and Consul Larkin named a little town on the Straits of Carquinez "Francisca" in honor of the first name of the wife of General Vallejo, went into executive session with himself and changed the name of Yerba Buena to "San Francisco." Upon*

hearing of Bartlett's maneuver, Semple and Larkin thereupon gave Senora Vallejo's second name–Benicia- to their projected metropolis.

EIGHTEEN

The Greatest Trees

February 1847

*She weren't more'n a thumbprint high
her first year
But was up to ninety-five feet on the day
they founded Carthage
And was at two hundred eighty when the
Romans built the Coliseum
Captain Beechey saw her at three
hundred seventy-nine*

In 1847, she was already an old lady when Napoleon said she'd never be felled because nobody made saws long enough to reach all the way across the trunk.

Just discharged from the California Battalion, Elam and Napoleon stood side by side to look up at the high branches of the gigantic tree.

Elam thought she looked like a mighty post God had put there to hold the sky up.

They didn't have trees like this back in Missouri, not even at Sylvester Paddy's sawmill. Why, the lowest branch was farther from the ground than the very tip-top of the trees in Missouri! And the trunk...why...the trunk didn't even look like it belonged to a tree! More like a wall somebody built around a cabbage patch.

[But Napoleon was wrong when he said they'd never cut her down because they didn't make saws long enough. He wasn't wrong much, but he sure was wrong that time, 'cause when they finally did cut her down forty-three years later, they didn't even use saws. Somebody cut her down a chip at a time with an almighty ax that didn't even mind how big the trunk was.

[In 1893, Dr. William P. Gibbons, curator of geology and mineralogy at the California Academy of Sciences in 1855, published a paper entitled *The Redwoods in the Oakland Hills* about a survey he had made to describe a "sea of stumps." In 1855, he had measured a stump "over 35 feet across at a height of four feet from the ground." (Mind that the diameter of the *General Sherman* tree, touted as the largest known living single stem tree on earth, measured only 32.6 feet across, including the bark. Dr. Gibbons' stump was 2.4 feet bigger, even back then.)

[The curator also described a later visit "...to the brow of a hill overlooking the Golden Gate...the relics of a redwood tree...showing nothing but a shell of wood and bark as a memorial of its past...within an area circumscribed by a wall of solid wood, the greatest diameter of which is thirty-five feet across at a distance of four feet from the ground...within this wonderful reception hall...I have had the pleasure of entertaining a goodly number of eminent men of science**...including John Muir...**"

[California Registered Historical Landmark No. 962 marks the site of the "Blossom Rock Navigation

Tree" in the Thomas J. Roberts Recreation Area, Redwood Regional Park, 11500 Skyline Boulevard.]

> *1847, February 22: The 4,759 man army of Major General Zachary Taylor battles the 18,530 man army of Antonio López de Santa Anna in the Battle of Buena Vista. Both sides sustained thousands of casualties.*

The wagons rolled down the ridgeline through a forest of trees smaller than the matriarchs; Napoleon's wagon in the lead, Elam's following. *The crowns of even these* lesser *trees would tower over the biggest ones in Missouri,* Elam marveled. They also saw a second *great* tree...not so great as the first, he thought...***but just give her another thousand years or so.***

Napoleon led his little group in their several wagons over the brow of that hill, then easterly into a pleasant swale bordered by a flowing brook. This was the place, he told his group, where he camped with his pal Mendenhall to fell lesser trees for whip-sawing into lumber.

To the east, a wide valley could be seen through the lower branches of those lesser trees, and a few structures (shacks, really). *Perhaps "lesser shacks" might be a better description: for they were crudely built of the partly rounded boards typically discarded as useless after being stripped of the round configuration preferred by God.* (Napoleon also maintained that those rustic boards of little value were variously called "log slabs" or "log siding."]

The great gold-mine of information that was Napoleon further explained that a thousand feet of lumber sawed to a thickness of two-an-a-half inches could be sold for a hundred and twenty-five dollars, quickening Elam's interest, for his purse had already "drawn low," as he put it.

Upon asking about the ownership of the land, he was told that the owners were farmers who disliked trees because the roots interfered so with the plow. "We wood-cutters," Napoleon said, smiling "are squatters."

> *1847, March 1: While placing a bet at a horse race held on a meadow near Mission Dolores, Leidesdorff became embroiled in an altercation with a man named McDougal. Leidesdorff was subsequently arrested by Alcalde George Hyde.*

> *1847, March 7: Fremont is ordered to report to General Kearny, who is passing out of the office of military governor. Kearny turns over his command to Colonel Richard B. Mason and orders Fremont to face charges of disobedience.*

> *March, 1847; Jasper O'Farrell is employed to lay out the "water-lots," which he did to the number of 444 between Rincon and Telegraph Hill, in size 45 feet 10 inches by 137 feet 6*

*inches.   Another   survey   was
subsequently made of 328 more lots by
O'Farrell*

There were, Elam considered, some few
advantages to becoming an old man. Because of that
occasionally desirable circumstance, he had been
assigned to the less strenuous task of pulling the whipsaw through the overhead log on the down-stroke,
thereby permitting the more strenuous task of up-
pulling the saw to be performed by such as the
youthful Napoleon. Still, a price was exacted: the
down-stroke person suffered from clouds of
descending sawdust, which filled the eyes, ears,
collars, and all other available apertures, On one such
occasion, while standing in sawdust up to his knees
and whistling dusty air from his nostrils, he recognized
a familiar voice hallooing a greeting: *Thomas!*

He hadn't seen his eldest son for four years, when
the boy trotted off to Oregon Country in 1843. Elam
dropped the saw handle, spat the sawdust from his lips
and scrubbed his fists in his eyes , then scrambled up
from the pit like a much younger man. He slowly and
silently approached his son with widespread arms, then
wrapped both arms about the boy with all his strength.

Boy! *Hardly a boy! Thomas would be, he guessed,
twenty-four years old!*

The son towered over the father: surely, one had
lengthened, the other shortened. Elam's eyes clouded a
bit, not from the sawdust. Still bound tightly together,
father and son stumbled to a nearby stump, arms
holding each other upright.

Son explained to father that he had arrived in San Francisco aboard the bark *Toulon* from Portland on the first available passage after receiving his father's letter about the purchase of a *Rancho*. "A *Rancho*," he said, choosing his words not so carefully, "can be dangerous ground."

No humor, Elam sighed. It was Thomas, all right. As serious as ever.

Thomas explained that he had dropped everything to come as quickly as possible to tell his father that it was of the absolute highest importance to build a house on the property as soon as possible, and to live in it *before* the war ends. There was a law (Preemption Act of 1841), he said, that would be become applicable if California should ever be annexed to the United States.

And pray God it will be.

Amazed that the casual system of posting letters worked as well as it did, Elam explained that he hadn't *actually hadn't* bought *a* rancho yet. Since Thomas had appeared so quickly, Elam now worried that others might also show up as quickly *and he'd have nothing to show them.*

> *1847, April 10: Lilburn Boggs, former governor of Missouri, is appointed to succeed John Nash as alcalde of the Sonoma District.*

Elam's worries continued to mount. While awaiting word about his potential purchase of a *rancho,* the irascible Napoleon Bonaparte Smith asked for his permission to marry Margeline. *Elam liked Napoleon very much and had no qualms about that marriage, but wasn't sure he could fathom a son-in-law called "Bony" by everyone. (Except the father-in-law.)*

Nevertheless, he quietly announced his approval in spite of some reluctance upon learning that Margeline had previously accepted the offer. After the proposed son-in-law passed on that bit of good news to his friend Bill Mendenhall, that *equally irascible soul* proposed marriage to Mary Allen!

A local newspaper subsequently reported:

One of the most beautiful marriages in the county was that by Alcalde *Burton of Mr. and Mrs. Napoleon Smith and Mr. and Mrs. William Mendenhall on April 18, 1847. Married in the Spring when the old Santa Clara Mission pear orchard was in bloom, the brides and grooms in their wedding clothes, followed by their friends, took a walk under the blossoming trees in the orchard. From Nature they had received a blessing...*

> *1847, April 29: Louis Keseberg, the last member of the Donner Party, arrives at Sutter's Fort.*

Activity settled like the sawdust in the whipsaw grounds on a rainy day after Thomas returned to Portland and Napoleon arrived from Santa Clara with his new bride. Running low on patience and unnerved by all the wedding activity, Elam seized the opportunity to press the *Rancho* question to the new son-in-law.

Napoleon sped across the Bay to San Francisco on the very next lumber scow, returning to report that absolutely no progress had been made. Leidesdorff had other matters on his mind, Napoleon said: having recently purchasing *Sitka,* a side-wheel steamer. The very first steamboat on San Francisco Bay, *Sitka* turned out to be a drastic mistake, for she was so underpowered as to be unable to make a proper headway against the wind in a bay famous for its wind. Then, on a trip up-river to Sutter's Fort during a down-river-wind day, the exasperated passengers deserted the slow boat, to walk the rest of the way, to arrive at Sutter's well ahead of the steamer.

Napoleon also reported that he thought Leidesdorff looked to be ill, which news was more than a little unsettling to Elam, who then felt ill himself. He had, after all, sent letters to everyone in the Brown Party, encouraging them to come to the Redwoods. So far, only Thomas had responded, which was alarming of itself. *What if no one else came? Alternately, what if they did and he had no* rancho *to show them?*

Leidesdorff, Napoleon elaborated, also had been assigned additional responsibilities in the workings of the City of San Francisco. Upon the resignation of *alcalde* Edwin Bryant, George Hyde was appointed as a replacement. Hyde named Leidesdorff not only to serve on the *ayuntamiento* [Town Council], but also assigned to him the position of City Treasurer.

> *The fine dust-soil of California washed down from the high mountains to the great rivers south and north, funneled into the delta, turned west to the Yerba Buena Cove, mingled into great swirls on the bedrock of that jelly bowl some 225 feet below; while clear water*

> *surged to the blue Pacific, men added*
> *more of the wet jelly-dust already in the*
> *bowl, capping the under-water softness*
> *with yet more softness, raising the*
> *surface even higher before adding giant*
> *structures to the mass already existing,*
> *to make it sink and sag and lean into the*
> *geological gruel belowl. [Later called*
> *"Bay Mud."]*

Napoleon also reported that Hyde discovered that the law allowed him, as *alcalde,* to sell lots in San Francisco for $12.00 each; **even those located *beneath* the waters of San Francisco Bay. (So-called "water lots." An auction was held from July 20-23, 1847. It was later determined that, because San Francisco had never been constituted a pueblo, the city fathers had no right to sell the land, and that the lots were illegal.)** [A U.S. Land Commission ruled in 1854, however, that San Francisco should have been considered to be a pueblo; the grants made by the *alcalde* were therefore legalized.] The lots, under water or not, were then re-sold to cronies at large profits. It was reported that Leidesdorff sold his grand house on the hill to raise more money to buy more lots, many of which sold for much more than $12.00: already, he owned more than three hundred lots!

Napoleon had just finished reciting his tale of woe when the worst happened: *a sizeable group arrived in the camp from Chiles' Ranch.*

Three wagons rolled in, bearing John and Mary Jones, the widow Margaret Allen, her son Josiah, daughter Melissa, grandbaby Jane, and daughter

Rebecca with *her* husband Wesley Bradley. All were full of questions about "his" *Rancho.* To still the tumult, he found a temporary respite by convincing the men that they should learn the art of whip-sawing lumber. To the boys, he suggested they might split short redwood logs to make roofing shingles.

> *1847, August 7: General Winfield Scott and 14,000 troops begin an offensive against Mexico City.*

On the eighth of August, Napoleon at last announced that the embattled Leidesdorff had found a *rancho* in the *Contra Costa,* three-quarters of a league in size, which had become available. Although delighted by the news, Elam would have preferred a larger one for he was currently worried that if everyone responded to his letters, he might not have found *enough* land for them all. A league, he recalled, measured *about* 4,000 acres. This *rancho,* then, would contain some 3,000 acres. *Not too bad. Not as big as the Vatican, maybe. But not bad, either.*

In any case, the size wasn't the looming problem.

Leidesdorff, Napoleon said, asked a thousand dollars for the *rancho,* about twice as many dollars Elam had left.

He wondered if it might be possible to negotiate a lower price, but after discussions with Napoleon, he decided the price wasn't negotiable.

He *did have* a thousand dollars due him from the sale of the property in the Platte, but he didn't have that money *now,* when he needed it.

Many were those that had headed west, but turned around and headed back.

It was said they "had seen the elephant."

Elam peered about, but saw no elephants.

NINETEEN

Benicia

August 1847

Elam kept a wary eye out, but no elephants arrived during the night, either. The night proved to be a long period of wakefulness; when he at last aroused himself, if that be the correct term, he felt very low and hardly able to cope with the son-in-law. Worse, Napoleon didn't sympathize one whit about the failure of the elephants, but continued to rave about Leidesdorff's *rancho,* if indeed it *was* his, declaring that the *rancho,* fictional or not, lay along the road to Benicia.

In addition, as if by the purest of coincidences, Napoleon added that it suddenly had become important to at once deliver a wagon-load of lumber to, of all places, Benicia!

Elam could hardly have cared less about Napoleon's need to deliver a load of lumber somewhere. But before he could draw a breath, Napoleon began to describe the route in great detail, emphasizing the necessity to pass the house of the widow Bernal. *Whoever* she *might be.* When you pass her house on Moraga's *rancho*, Napoleon told him, you'll be on Leidesdorff's *rancho. It had become* Leidesdorff's *rancho.*

Elam had no desire to even *look* at a *rancho* he couldn't afford to buy.

Napoleon slowed, as if he had become aware of Elam's reservations. At last, he declared with greatly muted passion that the delivery of lumber would simply...have...to...wait.

The late delivery would then be Elam's fault.

Then Napoleon raced on, his eyes glistening, perhaps sensing a potential victory. Leaping back into the fray with a "fantastic" idea: Margaret Allen, he said, on her trip from Chiles' *rancho,* had only yesterday passed along the *very same* road past the widow Bernal's house! She could go with Elam to point the way!

Elam struggled to find more reasons not to go, but Napoleon let loose with another volley: *his father-in-law, he said,* sneaking in the family tie, *could use his best delivery wagon! And his best team of fast mules!*

Elam was ready to give up the fight. Napoleon had so successfully re-worded the journey that it had now become a favor to the son-in-law!

The elephants headed back to the herd.

They drove the *best* wagon with the *best* mules most of the morning, but the widow wasn't home when they arrived at her house. Indeed, it appeared she hadn't been home for some time. Nevertheless, they chose to rest before her house [3662 Happy Valley Road] and to sample the water from her storied spring, which Napoleon had claimed to be of superior quality.

He had also said that he had been told by Leidesdorff that, upon passing the widow's house, one would have left Moraga's *rancho* and be on the *Rancho Acalanes.*

What did it matter? Why should Elam be interested in a rancho he wasn't able to afford in the first place?

But he looked around for signs of ownership such as fences, anyway. And saw none. The lonely adobe simply sat in a field at the side of a road, the spring its only companion.

It didn't matter. The spring water was plentiful, cold, and delicious. The spring might be a good omen, but omens don't buy ranchos.

Margaret, in spite of her supposed knowledge of the route, had no idea how much farther along the road it might be to Benicia. But that mattered little: struck by the view of the smooth golden hills all about them, they continued northerly at the best mule pace, until they arrived at the foot of a small valley ranging easterly. The valley was so inviting that the mules themselves decided to call a halt, pausing in the shade of a small grove of oaks. [Happy Valley Road.]

To the north, to the east, and to the south, a range of high, steep hills arced around the little valley *as if the Maker had curled his mighty protective arm about this very special place.*

Another omen?

The soft hills, blanketed with golden grass at this time of year, tall enough to tickle the bellies of the mules, gave promise that the little golden valley had great promise: to be so lush at this time of the year, the grass would need to have grown lush and strong and green.

Yet another omen? Elam recalled the immense grassy valley they had thankfully encountered after the crossing of the high mountains after leaving Johnson's Ranch.

A "branch," as they called a small stream in Missouri, coursed southerly along the westerly side of *the road. Would be a "*Permanente*" as they called a year-round stream in California? Surely, Elam conclude, the Maker wouldn't have curled his almighty arm about such a perfect place if He hadn't the water to make the grass so tall. Like the widow Bernal's spring, he thought.*

Could it all be too *perfect? Like the land on the Platte; perfect until the surveyors came along with their clever compasses and chains, dividing the land into Jefferson's Sections, no matter where the water was?*

"No," he told himself: here there would be no Section lines creating the infamous "land net" to carve away the water. In this place, they made property lines follow the land not the direction pointed out by the compass.

It was difficult to leave this magic place, but leave they must: there was lumber to be delivered. The road climbed the easy hills to the north, and they were pleased to find a succession of small lakes along the top of the ridge, testifying to the ready availability of water in the area. Ahead they could see the little village called "Martinez" beside the great river they knew to be called *Sacramento.*

A scow, large enough to accommodate the wagon *and* the fast mules, awaited them at the river, commanded by the tallest man Elam had ever seen; such a giant of a man that it appeared he might be able to vault the wide *Sacramento* with a single stride. He nodded to Margaret as if he recognized her, and perhaps he did. The flat-bottomed scow tipped to the point of overturning when the heavy wagon-load of lumber and the fast mules boarded; the man-mountain put one foot on her gunwale to steady her.

Two *Californios waited* aboard the boat, apparently deck hands, found no need to even pause their ceaseless conversation to push the dock away from the boat. When all were smoothly a-sail on the broad river, the deckhands rattled on. Astern, the humble houses of the little town of Martinez slowly retreated, probably thankful for the growing silence.

Upon arriving on the other side of the river at the quiet place (until they arrived) presumed to be Benicia, Elam led the mules and the still attached wagon from the boat. The very moment all found themselves fully aground, the day shattered into a thousand bits when a wildly galloping horse and rider, both clad in the same shade of darkest black, thundered up before them, causing even the *Californios* to force a regretful pause. Margaret and Elam gasped in unison when the black-clad rider deftly slid to the ground before a pair of exceedingly nervous mules,

Unbelievingly, the honorable Lilburn W. Boggs, former governor of Missouri, stared at them !

They hadn't seen the governor since a chance encounter on the trail at Steamboat Springs, when he very generously shared a dose of *Caminative Balsam* with a very ailing John Allen.

Nattily attired in a well-fitted black suit and a black string tie precisely centered in a sparkling white collar, the governor broke out a wide politician's smile on the handsome governor face as if he were campaigning to be President of the United States..

A rapid conversation ensued; even the *Californios* were impressed. Elam recalled that Boggs was the type of person seeming to be always in a great hurry. Obviously more interested in the ladies than the gentlemen, he began a questioning of Margaret, totally ignoring Elam. Upon learning that she had lost her husband on the trail at the Little Sandy River, however, the smiling face dissolved into the deepest of sympathies, then just as quickly recovering with a new smile that put the first one to shame.

Full smile intact, the governor diverted his attention to Elam, as if to say, "if not her husband, then just might **you** *might be, sir?"*

Elam reacted with his customary caution, which had no influence whatsoever over Boggs' rapid-fire manner, explaining that he, as well, had lost a spouse.

The conversation slowed for a moment. Then the political smile returned, changed again, altering the ex-governor's entire demeanor. Now he was cheerful. He straitened his perfectly straight tie, puffed out his chest and lit his face with yet *another* smile that proclaimed *he might go for the presidency after all.*

With both thumbs thrust into the little pockets of the presidential black vest, without even the slightest hint of braggadocio, he allowed that he, of all people, **just happened to be** the new *alcalde* for the very district in which they presently stood!

Furthermore, Boggs continued, *it happened that, at this moment, he was not otherwise occupied, and would therefore be most pleased to advise as to any proposals for his service as alcalde that might be outstanding.*

The conversation came to an abrupt halt.

Elam understood the point. He remained absolutely silent.

Margaret stood beside him, quiet as a post.

Even the *Californios* shut up.

The towering ferryman didn't dare breathe.

The silence lasted interminably.

Then, *alcalde* Lilburn Boggs, ever the mover, moved. Pressing Elam's hands into those of Margaret, he was obviously well pleased that the hands remained together. He waved the silent *Californios* to stand one on either side of the muted couple. *One needed witnesses for that which was about to occur, whether said witnesses understood English or not. Who's to know? Perfect witnesses.*

The faintest of waves signaled the breathless ferryman to position himself directly behind the couple. The fast mules, still tethered to the loaded wagon, understood their societal places and halted even their interminable scraping and shuffling of hooves.

The governor spoke. **When the governor, ex or not, speaks, all will please pay attention.**

Overhead, a squadron of seagulls fled noiselessly.

The governor whispered, in the softest of voices, that there would be no charge for the service.

In actual fact, there *was* a charge, but without objection. On that extremely fateful tenth day of August in the year of our Lord one thousand eight hundred and forty-seven, Elam Brown and Margaret Allen became man and wife. (The *alcalde* collected his usual fee: a trademark kiss from the bride.)

The world could breathe again. At least, the ferryman breathed. After all: he had a ferry to run. He nodded the *Californios* back to the boat for a cast-off.

The officiating *alcalde* moved quickly, not unusual
for him: he bowed, grabbed another kiss from the bride
before the groom could argue about overcharging,
apologized for a necessarily sudden departure with the
age-old lament that his busy political office required
his important and immediate presence elsewhere, and,
with a final wave, leaped aboard the departing
ferryboat.

The congregation gone, the newly-weds might
have wondered a bit about what they had just done, but
were disturbed because they hadn't yet done that
which they had actually come to Benicia to do

So, with great determination, they delivered the
lumber and raced back to the river to catch the last
ferry of the day to Martinez.

Heading back to the redwoods, it was necessary to
pass the magical place with the comforting hills and
the tall grass. Things were different now. Elam pulled
the mules off the road.

It was time for confession.

He began by wearily admitting that he shouldn't
have come to Benicia in the first place. For that, he
blamed Napoleon for insisting that he desperately
needed someone to deliver a stupid load of lumber
there.

Upon arriving at Benicia, they ran into the fast-
talker Lilburn Boggs, who smoothly married them
almost before they knew what was going on, and
without even asking them if they *wanted* to get
married.

Anyway, *it probably wasn't a* real *wedding,* he said
to Margaret. Although Boggs pronounced them man

and wife, he hadn't even made a note of it; Elam was sure there should be some sort of paper work, never mind the apparent lack of an official government. In addition, the witnesses wouldn't have understood what was said. There was only the ferryman, and he'd probably forgotten all about it by now.

They could each go their own separate ways and forget about the wedding.

Maybe it hadn't really happened.

Biting his tongue, he confessed all the rest of it: he had no money, and was unable to buy the rancho. *If there had actually* been *a wedding, she would have married a poor old man who had not the slightest idea what he would do next.*

The confession complete, he looked at her to see her reaction.

She smiled!

Then she double-tapped his folded hands.

She told him that Isaac had saved up money to buy a farm in Oregon Country.

He won't need it now.

No. Elam thought. He couldn't do this.

He couldn't take his best friend's wife for his *wife.*

And then take his best friend's money.

Like Boggs, she wouldn't listen.

"You need a wife," she said. "And I need a husband."

The mules smiled.

TWENTY

El Diseño

[The Map]

August 1847–February 1848

It was easy to sense trouble just by the way Napoleon sat on a tree stump.

Obviously waiting for them to return from Benicia, he didn't even rise from the stump to greet them.

It was easy to think something had gone very wrong.

Napoleon couldn't have known that they had run into the former governor of Missouri, and that they were now married to each other. He could see that the wagon was empty, that the load of lumber had been delivered. And that the fast mules looked just as fine as before. Elam clambered down from the wagon seat, then circled around behind the wagon to help Margaret down.

He nodded to Napoleon, who nodded back without rising from the stump or speaking or changing the expression on his face.

It just wasn't like Napoleon. Elam's heart sank.

At last, Napoleon spoke. He said he had been to San Francisco and talked with Leidesdorff, who was angry because Elam hadn't responded to his *rancho* offer. Leidesdorff was offering it around to others.

Elam's heart sank further.

Just when it seemed that, at last, all had changed for the better.

But he didn't even know how much money Margaret had, because she couldn't read.

Maybe there was enough.

Maybe not.

She signaled him to climb up into the rear of her wagon and to sit on a large wooden trunk that she dusted off for him. Reaching to the floor behind the trunk, she produced what appeared to be a small child wrapped in swaddling clothes. His eyes widened; he flinched when she gingerly placed the bundle on his lap.

At last, he placed his hands on either side of the bundle and found it to be surprisingly rigid. Unable to delay any longer, he slowly and carefully unrolled the swaddling clothes.

And found a clock.

A very beautiful wooden clock it was; weighing heavy on his lap. His gaze shifted repeatedly from the clock to Margaret, pleading for an explanation. At last, she leaned forward, opened the hinged door covering the clock face. A paper envelope lurked there, tucked behind the pendulum.

She smiled and signaled again, which he took to be a message to extract the envelope from the clock.

Inside was a thin wad of bills.

There weren't many.

But there was enough.

Four hundred and forty dollars. *Americano.*

He breathed again.

Thank God!

Next morning, Elam handed a thousand wrinkled dollars to his son-in-law, with instructions to take the money to his friend Leidesdorff at once.

When Napoleon returned later in the afternoon, he reported that Leidesdorff had accepted the money without comment, which, Napoleon explained, wasn't unusual for him. Neither had Leidesdorff offered a receipt, which, Elam assumed, wasn't unusual, either. Before Elam could raise the question, his son-in-law went on to say that Leidesdorff had placed a good order for a quantity of lumber to be sold to the city for sidewalk construction.

Elam assumed such a large order might have been grounds for termination of the discussion about such things, so he let the question lie; especially when Napoleon suggested that he might assist in the whipsawing of the lumber; his purse had grown thin indeed after giving Leidesdorff most of his money.

Much of the demand for lumber came from San Francisco, located just across the Bay from the lumber camp in the *San Antonio* redwoods. As a seaport, San Francisco was perfectly located because of the Bay. As a city, however, not so perfect; most of the flat land was already occupied, and the city's steep hills made development impossibly difficult.

It was well-noted that *Yerba Buena Cove* was relatively shallow. An Irish surveyor named Jasper O'Farrell was hired to draw up a plan for dividing the fledgling city into streets and lots, including the shallow portion in the *Cove*. The accommodating O'Farrell didn't label them "under-water lots," which might diminish the value; instead, they were labeled "water-lots," a significantly better title, avoiding the problem of explaining to prospective purchasers that they were unusable.

A second problem remained: the erstwhile steep lots remained steep. It was ultimately determined that the problem could be solved by simply grading the steep lots level. That gave rise to a third problem: what to do with the excess dirt generated by the solution to the second problem?

It could be seen that the solution to the third problem might be to re-locate the second problem's resultant dirt to the first problem, for those lots were still under-water.

The city fathers were beside themselves with delight: *They could actually* create *land; something which, heretofore, could only be accomplished by God!*

Under Mexican law, a fourth problem was raised, in that a strip of beach and harbor must be reserved for the exclusive use by the government and could not, therefore, be sold. *Even if created by the government.* As a result, numerous illegal lots were sold for the token amount price of $12 each: the fourth problem was solved by simply ignoring the law.

> *In many places within the business portion of the Cove lie large vessels, which in disastrous years got stranded or were used as store-ships or lodging houses on the beach. These ships remained where they lay, fast imbedded in mud, while long streets, hollow beneath, and numerous buildings, arise on every side, effectually hemming them in forever.*

To the great delight of all, Warren Brown arrived in the redwood forest on the first day of September. As upon the arrival of Thomas back in April, Elam was in his usual position in the pit at the lower end of the saw. He hadn't seen the boy since leaving him to recuperate from trail sickness at Ft. Bridger over a year ago. *Boy? Did he think* boy? *Like Thomas, hardly a boy anymore: more a man: probably twenty-one years old, already!*

The *boy* looked well. Ft. Bridger's dry climate had obviously worked its wonders, as they'd hoped it might. When he arrived in Portland on the sixth of July, he said, found a job in a cooperage. On another lucky day, he had, by sheer chance, run into his brother Thomas.

Elam gratefully handed him the handle of the whipsaw, accepted somewhat hesitantly, but gracefully, by Warren.

The clan was gathering. Would there be a rancho?

He had written the letters and the family responded. First, Thomas, even if only to advise. Then John and Mary Jones, Josiah, Melissa, Rebecca, Wesley, Jane. *And Margaret, of course.* Warren's arrival completed the assemblage.

All would be lost if the war ended before the rancho *question was resolved.*

Still, his arms ached from the whipsawing: the interminable whipsawing. Whipsawing was young-man's work, and it had been oh-so-long-ago that he had been a young man. The money was pretty good, though: his purse had drawn low, as the New Englanders said.

Napoleon arrived in the darkest hour, a full Napoleonic smile plastered across his face right up to his eyes.

"Hello, Bony," Elam managed to choke out that day. He raised himself to his fullest available height and spoke in a tone he had never before used with his likeable son-in-law.

His voice aquiver, Elam forcefully demanded *demanded, mind you,* to know *when they'd get a response from Bony's old friend Leidesdorff.*

Just...like...that.

Bony nodded.

He'd report back, he said.

> *1847, September 12: General Winfield Scott orders the bombardment of Chapultepec castle, the last major defense before Mexico City. The war was very near its end.*

On the following day, Napoleon anxiously reported that an election was to be held in accordance with Governor Mason's ordinance to select six persons to constitute an *ayuntamiento,* a town council of San Francisco, until the end of the year 1848. This would, he said, replace the *ayuntamiento* appointed July 28 by *alcalde* George Hyde.

Napoleon added that he was sure Leidesdorff would consider that election far more significant than any other matters in which he might be involved. Having been duly elected to the Council, Leidesdorff was also chosen to serve as treasurer, and was additionally placed on a committee assigned to the exploration of measures necessary for the establishment of a public school.

Elam was staggered. Surely, the *Great Man* Leidesdorff would be far too busy to deal with such a little matter as a *rancho.*

The Council entered with great spirit upon the duties of office by passing a multitude of laws; one of which rescinded an existing condition relative to the sale of lots which required the fencing and construction of a building within a year of purchase. That condition had served to mightily limit purchases of lots; the recision greatly encouraged speculation, for purchasers could then hold an indefinite number of lots without requirements to erect buildings or fences on them. Speculators (including Council members) thereafter employed the practice of using "straw men," friends and cronies, to take title to lots snapped up by them at the regulated price of $12.00, which would then be resold at greatly inflated prices, under water or not.

> *1847, September 14: American soldiers under General Winfield Scott raise the Stars and Stripes over the National Palace of Mexico. For all practical purposes, the war was over.*

Fully occupied with his duties on the *ayuntamiento* and his several positions as treasurer and new member of the School Board as well as the new possibilities of profit from potential sales of city lots recently acquired, Leidesdorff understandably might have had little interest in an urgent need to quickly convey the *rancho* he had purchased (with Elam's money) to Elam, or even to acknowledge the fact that he had purchased the *rancho* himself.

Now at the point of nervous exhaustion and, on the other hand, with very limited knowledge with even the status of the war with Mexico, but with the full realization that it was necessary to hold full title to the property *before* the end of the war, Elam became exceedingly overwrought. This, Napoleon understood, but could do little about.

Meantime, Elam busied himself by doubling or tripling his output of whip-sawed lumber. However, it is possible that powers-at-be took mercy on him; the sky clouded over and heavy early rains commenced in the forest, halted work entirely, which did much for his aching body but little enough for his frayed mind.

At last, Napoleon delivered to Elam, on November 10, 1847, a fully executed *titulo* that transferred title of the *Rancho Acalanes* in the *Contra Costa* from Wm. A. Leidesdorff to Señor Elam Brown, attested to by First *Alcalde* George Hyde. [4 DEEDS 317]

Elam set the document aside when Napoleon, without further explanation, thrust an earlier document into his shaking hands:

> *1847, September 2: Rancho Acalanes titulo: Candelario Valencia to Guillermo Leidesdorff, Book A, pages 7-8, Spanish Records, Municipality of San Francisco. [4 Deeds 316]*

The Lord be praised! Elam vowed to build Him a church.

TWENTY-ONE

Nous voila, Lafayette!

[Lafayette, We Are Here!]

January-February 1848

1848, January 24: James W. Marshall discovers gold at Sutter's Mill in Coloma. Sutter with-holds news of the discovery.

1848, February 2: The Treaty of Guadalupe Hidalgo is signed by President Polk, ending the War between the United States of America and the Mexican Republic. The US will pay $15 million to Mexico and receive California, a portion of New Mexico, most of Arizona, Nevada and Utah, parts of Wyoming, and an agreement on the location of the border with Texas.

Late in the afternoon of February 7, 1848, three wagons pulled up at the magical place on the road to Benicia where Margaret declared that Elam needed a wife and she needed a husband. The special little valley was even more beautiful than on the day of the declaration: God had spent the winter months wetting the place down for them, coloring the brown grass a luscious green, growing it fence-post high.

In the first wagon, driven by Elam, rode the men: Elam, Warren and Margaret's son Josiah.

The second wagon contained the ladies: Margaret at the helm, Melissa and Elizabeth Jane in the van.

No passengers rode in the remaining wagon. Driven by the sawyer William Davis and heavily laden with freshly whip-sawed redwood lumber, there could be no room for passengers. On arrival, the men converged on Davis's wagon for the unloading, to allow him time to return to the San Antonio redwoods before nightfall.

Pre-cut by Davis in accordance with Elam's specifications, the parts were laid out on the grass in an order dictated by Elam for the construction of a house that Thomas had indicated might be necessary to satisfy a legal requirement that they had actually in the place. The house wouldn't be very big, but Elam hoped it would be big enough. Simple enough to construct, it would consist of a frame at the top, bottom, and corner: walled with pre-cut boards nailed vertically to the frame.

Warren and Josiah worked frantically with Elam to erect the house before nightfall. They had successfully raised the walls when Margaret announced that supper was ready and already growing cold.

After choking down the meal, the men raced back to complete installation of the roof, managing to complete that task just before dark.

Afterward, Elam claimed that "he built the house while Margaret cooked dinner."

He might have claimed to add the roof while Margaret did the dishes.

There was, in fact, no floor in the house but the green grass. Margaret did say that she hoped to, someday, have a house with a floor.

1848, March 15: The Californian reports on the discovery of gold, but most people are skeptical.

1848, May 12: The first convincing announcement of the discovery of gold occurred when Sam Brannan ran through the streets of San Francisco, a bottle of gold dust in his hand, shouting **"Gold! Gold! Gold from the American River!**

The End

Margaret Allen Brown's clock

AFTERWORD

1848, May 18: William A. Leidesdorff, $50,000 in debt, dies *intestate* at the age of thirty-six, three months after the Browns settle on the Rancho Acalanes. Cause of death cited variously as brain fever, stroke, meningitis, typhus, pneumonia, suicide, or murder.

1850, September 9: California becomes the 31st State of the Union.

1856, November 26: Final Decree, Rancho Acalanes.

1857, January 15: Rancho surveyed by Andrew J. Coffee: 3,328.25 acres

1857, March 12: La Fayette Post Office approved.

1968, July 29: City of Lafayette incorporated.

SELECTED BIBLIOGRAPHY

Abeloe, Father William N. *The History of Mission San Jose California.* Fresno: Academy Library Guild, 1958.

Allen, Eleanor. *Canvas Caravans.* Portland: Binfords & Mort, 1946.

Allen, Ethel E. *A Narrative of Events in the Lives of the Descendants of William Allen.* Salem: Monograph, 1847.

Allen, Glenn B. *Allen Papers.* Monograph.

Allen, Samuel A. *A Brief Biography of the Allen Family.*

Bagwell, Beht. *Oakland The Story of a City.* Novato: Presidio Press, 1982.

Bain, David Haward. *Empire Express, Building the First Transcontinental Railroad.* New York: The Penguin Group, 1999.

Bancroft, Hubert Howe. *History of California.* San Francisco: The History Company, 1886.

Bancroft, Hubert H. *History of Oregon, 1848-1888.* San Francisco: The History Company, 1888.

Bancroft, Kim. *Literary Industries, 1890 (Abridged).* San Francisco: Heyday Books, 2013.

Bancroft Library, Berkeley, California

Bauer, K. Jack. *The Mexican War, 1846-1848.* New York: Macmillan Publishing Co., Inc., 1974.

Beebe, Rose Marie. *Lands of Promise and Despair.* Berkeley: Heyday Books, 2001.

Bernier, Oliver. *Lafayette.* New York: E.P. Dutton, Inc., 1983.

Bidwell, John. *Life in California before the Gold Discovery.* Palo Alto: Lewis Osborne, 1966.

Bidwell, John. *The First Emigrant Train to California,* Century Magazine, 1890.

Bidwell, General John. *Echoes of the Past.* Chico: The Chico Advertiser, 1864.

Bowman, Isaiah. *Well-Drilling Methods.* Washington: Government Printing Office, 1911.

Bray, A.F. *Elam Brown Opposes Dueling in Contra Costa.* Oakland: Monograph, February 15, 1937.

Brown, Thomas A. *Thomas A. Brown Papers.* Martinez: Contra Costa County Library

Buck, Rinker. *The Oregon Trail.* New York: Simon & Schuster, 2015.

Burgess, S.D. 1951. The forgotten redwoods of the East Bay. *California Historical Quarterly,* March 1951, pp.6-19

Burnett, Peter H. *An Old California Pioneer.* Oakland: Biobook, 1946 (Reprint)

Carranco, Lynwood. *Logging the Redwoods.* Caldwell: The Caxton Printers, Ltd., 1975

Caughey, John Walton. *The California Gold Rush.* Berkeley: University of California Press, 1948.

Chaffin, Tom. *Pathfinder.* New York: Hill and Wang, 2002.

Clackamas County Surveyor's Office, Oregon City, Oregon

Coffman, Lloyd W. *Blazing a Wagon Trail to Oregon.* Enterprise: Echo Books, 1993.

Contra Costa County Historical Society, Martinez, California

Contra Costa Gazette. *Life Sketches of Elam Brown.* Martinez: Contra Costa Gazette, 1879.

Contra Costa County Library, Pleasant Hill, California

Cotteral, Jack. *Lafayette Community Church, A History.* Lafayette: Lafayette United Methodist Church, 2005.

Crisman, Kevin J. *When Horses Walked on Water: Horse Powered Ferries in the Nineteenth Century.* Washington: Smithsonian Institution Press, 1999.

Davis, William Heath. *Seventy-five Years in California.* San Francisco: John Howell, 1929.

De Veer, *The Story of Rancho San Antonio,* Oakland: Published by the Author, 1924.

DeVoto, Barnard. *The Year of Decision 1846.* New York: Little, Brown and Company, 1942.

Dodds, J.S. *Original Instructions Governing Public Land Surveys 1815-1855.* Ames: Powers Press, 1944.

Dunning, Joan. *From the Redwood Forest.* White River Junction: Chelsea Green Publishing Company, 1998.

Farquhar, Francis P. *History of the Sierra Nevada.* Berkeley, University of California Press, 1965.

Freeman, Leslie J., PhC. *Alameda County Past & Present.* San Leandro: San Leandro Reporter , 1946..

Gibbons, W.P. *Erythea 1:161-166.* The Redwoods in the Oakland Hills. 1893

Gilbert, Bil. *Westering Man The Life of Joseph Walker.* New York: Atheneum, 1983

Gillis, Michael J. *John Bidwell and California.* Spokane: The Arthur H. Clark Company, 2003.

Hale, John. *Elam Brown-Pioneer.* Kentfield: Monograph, 1995.

Hale, John. *Descendants of Elam Brown.* Kentfield: Monograph.

Hamilton, Oscar Brown. *History of Jersey County, Illinois.* Springfield: Munsell Publishing, 1919.

Hammond, George P. *The Weber Era in Stockton History.* Berkeley: The Friends of the Bancroft Library, 1982.

Hastings, Lansford W. *The Emigrants' Guide, to Oregon and California.* Cincinnati: George Conclin, 1845.

Hecox, Margaret M. *California Caravan.* San Jose: Harlan-Young Press, 1966.

Hittell, Theodore H. *History of California.* San Francisco: N.J. Stone & Company, 1897.

Holmes, Philip. *Two Centuries at Mission San Jose, 1797-1997.* Fremont: Museum of Local History, 1997.

Holliday, J.S. *The World Rushed In.* New York: Simon and Schuster, 1981.

Hoover, Mildred Brooke, et al. *Historic Spots in California.* Stanford: Stanford University Press, 1932.

Howard, Thomas Frederick. *Sierra Crossing, First Roads to California.* Berkeley: University of California Press, 1998.

Hulaniski, F.J. *History of Contra Costa County.* Berkeley: Elms Publishing Co., 1917.

Illinois State Historical Society. *Publications.* Springfield: Phillips Brothers, 1904.

Jones, Mary A. *Recollections of Mary A. Jones.* Alamo: Monograph, 1915.

Johnson, Overton, & Winter, Wm. H. *Across the Rocky Mountains.* Lafayette, Ind.: John B. Semans, Printer , 1846.

Kimball, Sandy. *La Fayette, A Pictorial History.* Lafayette: Lafayette Historical Society, 1976.

Lafayette Historical Society, Lafayette, California

Lamson, Joseph. *Round Cape Horn.* Bangor: Press of O.F. & W.H. Knowles, 1878.

Langelier, John. *A History under Spain and Mexico, 1776-1846.* Denver: U.S. Department of the Interior, 1992.

Lass, William E. *Navigating the Missouri.* University of Oklahoma Press, Norman, 2008

Lavender, David. *California, Land of New Beginnings.* New York: Harper & Row, 1972.

Lewis, Donovan. *Pioneers of California.* San Francisco: Scottwall Associates, 1993.

Lewis, Oscar. *Sutter's Fort: Gateway to the Gold Fields.* Englewood Fields: Prentice-Hall, 1966.

Library of Congress, Washington, DC 27th *Congress, Ch 16, 5 Stat. 453 (1841)*

Lienhard, Heinrich. *From St. Louis to Sutter's Fort, 1846.* University of Oklahoma Press, Norman, 1961.

Lienhard, Heinrich. *A Pioneer at Sutter's Fort, 1846-1850.* The Calafia Society, Los Angeles, 1941.

Linn, E.A. & N. Sargent. *The Life and Public Services of Dr. Lewis F. Linn.* New York: D. Appleton & Company, 1857.

Lyman, George D. *John Marsh, Pioneer.* New York: The Chautauqua Press, 1931.

MacGregor, Greg. *Overland.* Albuquerque: University of New Mexico Press, 1996.

MacMullen, Jerry. *Paddle-Wheel Days in California.* Stanford: Stanford University Press, 1970.

Margolin, Malcolm. *The East Bay Out.* Berkeley: Heyday Books, 1974.

Mattes, Merrill J. *The Great Platte River Road.* Lincoln: Nebraska State Historical Society, 1969.

McCarthy, Francis Florence. *The History of Mission San Jose, California.* Fresno: Academy Literary Guild, 1958.

McGlashan, C.F. *History of the Donner Party.* Stanford: Stanford University Press, 1940.

McLynn, Frank. *Wagons West.* New York: Grove Press, 2002.

Meldahl, Keith Heyer. *Hard Road West.* Chicago: The University of Chicago Press, 2007.

Melendy, H. Brett. *The Governors of California, Peter H. Burnett to Edmund G. Brown.* Georgetown: The Talisman Press, 1965.

Morgan, Dale. *Overland in 1846.* Lincoln: University of Nebraska Press, 1993.

Multnomah County Surveyor's Office, Portland, Oregon

Munro-Fraser, J.P. *History of Contra Costa County, California.* San Francisco: W.A. Slocum & Co., 1882.

Murphey, Virginia Reed. *Across the Plains in the Donner Party.* Golden: Outbooks, 1980.

Mutnick, Dorothy G. *Some California Poppies & Even a Few Mommies Volume I.* Lafayette: Part Time Publications, 1980.

Mutnick, Dorothy G. *Some California Poppies & Even a Few Mommies Volume II.* Lafayette: Part Time Publications, 1980.

Neiderheiser, Leta Lovelace. *Jesse Applegate, a Dialogue with Destiny,* Mustang: Tate Publishing, 2010.

Nelson, Robert. *Enemy of the Saints.* Baltimore: Publish America, 2011.

Nunnis, Doyce B., Jr. *The Bidwell-Bartleson Party.* Santa Cruz: Western Tanager Press, 1991.

Olmsted, Roger R. *Scow Schooners of San Francisco Bay.* Cupertino: California History Center, 1988.

Paddison, Joshua. *A World Transformed.* Berkeley: Heyday Books, 1999.

Palgon, Gary Mitchell. *William Alexander Leidesdorff.* Atlanta: Palgon, 2005.

Perrin, William Henry, *History of Delaware County and Ohio.* Chicago: OL Baskin, 1882.

Peters, Ray, *The Lafitte Case,* Aurora: Write Way Publishing, 1997.

Phillips, Charles & Burnett, Betty. *Missouri, Crossroads of the Nation.* Sun Valley: American Historical Press, 2003.

Portland Historical Society, Portland, Oregon

Purcell, Mae Fisher. *History of Contra Costa County.* Berkeley: The Gillick Press, 1940.

Preston, Richard. *The Wild Trees.* New York: Random House. 2007.

Rarick, Ethan. *Desperate Passage.* New York: Oxford University Press, Inc., 2008.

Regnery, Dorothy. *The Battle of Santa Clara.* San Jose: Smith & McKay, 1977.

Richards, Rand. *Mud Blood and Gold.* San Francisco: Heritage House Publishers, 2009.

Robinson, John H., M.D. *A map of Mexico, Louisiana, and the Missouri Territory. 1819,* (G3300 ct1309,

Geography and Map Division, Library of Congress)

Sager, Catherine, *Across the Plains in 1844.* http://pressbooks.com, 2012

San Jose Evening News. *Battle of Santa Clara.* San Jose, February 9, 1917.

San Jose Evening News. *Survivors of the Battle.* San Jose, February 6, 1917.

San Jose Pioneer. *Elam Brown.* San Jose, January 26, 1878.

Scott-Applegate cutoff, www.oregonoverland.com

Shally, Gladys. *Elam Brown.* Monograph, 1965.

Sides, Hampton. *Blood and Thunder.* New York: Anchor Books, 2007.

Simmons, Edwin H., Brigadier General. *The Secret Mission of Archibald Gillespie.* Washington, D.C.: Marine Corps Association, 1968.

Soulé, Frank. *The Annals of San Francisco.* New York: D. Appleton, 1855.

Stewart, George R. *The Prairie Schooner Got Them There.* Rockville: Forbes, America Heritage Magazine, Vol. 13, Issue 2, 1962.

Stone, Irving. *Men to Match My Mountains.* New York: Berkley Books, 1956.

Storer, Tracy I. & Usinger, Robert L. *Sierra Nevada Natural History.* Berkeley: University of California Press, 1981.

Stuart, Reginald R. *San Leandro...a History.* San Leandro, First Methodist Church, 1951.

Surveyor General of the United States. *General Instructions to his Deputies.* (Facsimile) Detroit: W.W. Hart, Book & Job Printer, 1850.

The California Star, page 3. Yerba Buena, February 6, 1847.

University of Missouri Plat Map Collection, www.digital.library.umsystem.edu

Valencius, Conevery Bolton. *The Health of the Country.* New York: Basic Books, 2002.

Vouri, Michael. *The Pig War.* Friday Harbor: Basic Books, 2006.

Walker, Dale L. *Bear Flag Rising,* New York: A Forge Book, 1999.

Waugh, John C. *The Class of 1846.* New York: The Ballantine Publishing Group, 1999.

Weston Historical Museum, Weston, Missouri

Wills, Charles A. *A Historical Album of Oregon.* Brookfield: The Millbrook Press, 1995.

Young, Andrew H. *The Improvers of Lafayette.* Lafayette: Lafayette Historical Society, 1981

CPSIA information can be obtained
at www.ICGtesting.com
Printed in the USA
FSOW02n1743030917
38254FS